A Spirituality *of* Service

Reflections on a Life-Long Journey of Faith and Work Among the World's Poor

Jerry Aaker

Pfeifer-Hamilton Publishers
Middleton, Wisconsin

D1472253

Pfeifer-Hamilton Publishers
8665 Airport Rd
Middleton, WI 53562
www.pfeiferhamilton.com

A Spirituality of Service
Reflections on a Life-Long Journey of Faith
and Work Among the World's Poor

A Spirituality of Service is the initial title in the
Wisdom from the Elders series published by Pfeifer-Hamilton.

Scripture quotations are from the *Holy Bible, New Revised Standard
Version*, copyright 1989, Division of Christian Education of the National
Council of Churches of Christ in the U.S.A. Used by permission. All
rights reserved.

Editing: Susan Rubendall, Merrill Kempfert
Book design: Joy Morgan Dey
Cover photos: Robert P Engwall, Jerry Aaker

Printed in the United States of America

10 9 8 7 6 5 4 3 2 1

Library of Congress Control Number: 2012940382

ISBN: 978-1-935388-04-3

To Judy, my dearest companion,
intimate friend and wife, who has encouraged
and accompanied me on our journey together
for over forty-seven years.

Table of Contents

Foreword

"No one should spend so much time in contemplation that they ignore the needs of a neighbor, nor be so absorbed in action that they feel no need for contemplation of God." So wrote St. Augustine in *The City of God.*

The strength of this book is the way in which Jerry Aaker captures the heart of what St. Augustine espoused. He does this by dipping into his journals from several decades abroad with humanitarian agencies and giving us deeply personal impressions from his own journeys. He shares with us his partnership with people struggling against the odds to overcome some of the worst features of poverty in developing countries. He does this as a man of faith, who understands his work as a fruit of faith, and his walk with God as a foundation of strength for his work.

Aaker's love for people and his faith in Christ are palpable and interconnected. In short, his spirituality does not retreat from the harshness and joys of life, but emerges from this milieu and is all the more necessary because of it.

Spirituality is a maddeningly elusive term, one that can mean almost anything. So it is refreshing that Aaker anchors his spirituality in the faith confessed and nurtured by the church—*and practiced in the world.* That connection comes through consistently on these pages. Unlike most books on spirituality, this one was not written by a theologian or by someone who has practiced and taught spirituality in quiet surroundings—though such guides are not to be despised.

A Spirituality of Service was written by a layman who felt called by God to live and work among the poor and who also felt a need to undergird that work by learning to draw strength from God. As a result, the product is authentic. It is, as he admits, a "spirituality of imperfection," therefore easy for us imperfect folks to relate to. I say that with some conviction because my wife Shirley and I read the 35 chapters aloud together, a chapter each evening. We felt drawn to the people Aaker met, enriched by his own journey and grateful for the mutual reflection that it spawned.

Art Simon
Founder and President Emeritus
Bread for the World

Introduction

IN THESE PAGES I EXPLORE OUT LOUD with you my life-long quest to understand and live out the rich and varied elements of my own spirituality of service. I invite you to walk with me, as I reflect on how questions and explorations about spirituality have been tested and honed during my sojourn of 40 years working with people living in conditions of injustice and poverty in many countries around the world. My hope is that, as we walk together, you will find flashes of wisdom and insight that help you to understand your own spiritual journey with a new depth. My wish is that you will gain an increased appreciation for the mysteries that abound within the complexities of your own faith and practical applications for your daily life and work in service to others.

I am a lay person, not a trained theologian. This book is based on my experiences, both as a volunteer and a professional, in programs that work to end hunger, injustice and human suffering in the world.

You may ask, "Why another book on Christian spirituality?" Good question. Indeed there are many good books on this subject, mostly written by priests, nuns, pastors, theologians, scholars and teachers of prayer. These are good and helpful resources, and some of them are referenced in this book. Books on spirituality and prayer are written to provide guidance, instruction and the theological/historical basis of spiritual practices. The writers, as well as some of the audience for these books, are often full-time religious and ordained persons working in seminaries or monasteries, or they are spiritual directors and teachers. Also many resources give an overview of spiritual disciplines and offer practical suggestions for lay people, but few look at the interface between spirituality and action in the world, especially from the perspective of those who work directly with people living in poverty.

This book does not attempt to provide a comprehensive overview of spirituality. Rather, I try to present an honest account of how I employed spiritual practices and faith as integral to my work of service in many cultural contexts around the world. Mine is certainly a "spirituality of imperfection" to use the term coined by Wil Hernandez in *Henri Nouwen: A Spirituality of Imperfection*, his exhaustive study of Henri Nouwen, one of history's most prolific writers on topics of prayer, spirituality and faith.

The book covers a variety of themes encompassing service, faith and spiritual practices. The experiences are described as they happened, and the people written about in these reflections are real. These experiences intersect with my reflections and spiritual practices in the midst of these encounters. Besides my own reflections, I make use of wisdom from a variety of authors to support the themes of the book — especially Henri Nouwen, a Catholic priest, and Marjorie Thompson, a Presbyterian pastor, as well as other Catholic, Protestant and Quaker authors.

This is not a book about the organizations with which I worked; nor is it intended to fully explain how and for what purposes these organizations exist. Yet most of the reflections and stories come out of the context of work within these programs. Therefore, I include a glossary of these organizations and their websites for those interested in knowing more about them.

A basic premise of the book is that those engaged in service in the name of Christ, whether in congregations, human services or in missions of mercy, justice and human development, can be strengthened in their work by keeping themselves connected to God and grounded in the Spirit through the discipline of daily spiritual practices.

How to Use This Book

You will see that each chapter focuses on a distinct theme and concludes with a reflection on the subject matter, often with quotes from other authors, followed by a scripture text and a few questions. You can use the book in several ways. One is for personal learning, private devotions and meditation. Second, the material can be used for reflection and discussion in a group setting. After you have read each chapter, I suggest the following:

- First, reread the short reflection at the end of each chapter, watching for your reactions to the theme presented in the chapter as well as the thoughts put forth in the reflection.

- Meditate on the Scripture passage by reading it slowly several times; taking a few minutes of silence to notice what thoughts, images and prayers this text stirs in your heart. If you are reading this in private, you may want to keep a journal of your musings. In a group, individuals can share their thoughts and images aloud.

- Use the questions to stimulate thoughts and discernment. Again, in private this might lead to journaling or a time of silent meditation. In a group, allow everyone, if they are so inclined, to respond to the question(s). Allow some time for each person to share without interruption in an attitude of prayerful listening.

In either case, you do not need to read the chapters in the sequence in which they are printed in the book. You can pick and choose the themes that are most pertinent and interesting. For groups, this will depend on the number of sessions you plan to meet. For individual readers or for couples, I suggest that you read with patience, perhaps taking one chapter a day and using the Scripture and questions for daily devotions and reflection on your own spiritual journey.

Most likely, there are more themes and chapters than can be used during the typical cycle of a study or prayer group. Thus, consider several options and be flexible. For example, a study of the spiritual journey and personal disciplines might use several chapters from Part 1: The Journey and Part 5: Developing a Rule of Life. Or you may wish to have a series of sessions on spiritual practices by choosing five or six chapters from Part 2: Spiritual Practices. Select several chapters from Part 3: Spirituality in Action for a series on themes of service and action in the world. For themes and stories of faithful service, choose from Part 4: Encounters on the Journey—or mix and match any of the themes that particularly interest you.

Finally, here is a word about format. Journal entries identify the place and time, and they are presented here just as I wrote them many years ago. You may at times feel the need to seek more information about the context or situation. I purposefully do not fully describe or explain every situation or reference, hoping to leave you with a curiosity to explore more on your own. The book is not organized chronologically, as in a memoir, but by theme. Citations of other authors are noted in the text and listed in the bibliography.

People from all walks of life and many faiths are searching with renewed intensity for a spiritual center. Within traditional Christian communities, many speak of being on a "spiritual journey."

Marjorie Thompson, *Soul Feast*, p. 32

BEING ON A JOURNEY usually implies a starting and ending point—but our spiritual journey seems to never end. As a metaphor for the spiritual life, the term journey is modern and is not used in Scripture. Yet St. Paul presents a model as one who made many journeys and recorded the details in his letters to the young churches. We can learn from his example about the importance of commitment and perseverance on the journey.

These first chapters present something of my spiritual and geographic journeys and how journaling has been an important tool to help me clarify my understanding of faith, service and the spiritual life.

My Life: A Short History
of the Unexpected

We must be ready to allow ourselves to be interrupted by God.
God will constantly be crossing our paths and canceling our plans . . .

Dietrich Bonhoeffer

T HE RAW MATERIAL for this book comes from my journals. Rereading these journals refreshed my memories and reawakened my spirit as I recalled good people and experiences from my past. After going back over many years of my journals, I realize that my interest in spirituality emerged and grew as an integral part of my interest in holistic ministry and my work with people and communities in diverse settings. In my case, that meant Christian spirituality as related to the career of service I had felt called to and had chosen.

Travel and the pursuit of a life of service has been continuous ever since I went to England in 1960 for a year as a student volunteer at Hothorpe Hall, a Lutheran youth and conference center serving the European Lutherans who settled in Great Britain after World War II.

I was born into a family of Norwegian heritage and grew up on a small farm near Kenyon, Minnesota. In 1962 I graduated from Luther College in Iowa, where I began to think deeply about human development for the first time at the feet of my sociology professor, David Johnson, and I experienced spiritual mountaintops through singing and appreciating sacred music. Later, when I chose to go to Hawaii for graduate school, I was introduced to the cultures of Asia and the Pacific.

In Hawaii, Judy and I were married and began our journey together. During her studies to become a registered nurse at Lutheran Deaconess Hospital in Minneapo-

2

lis, she had dreamed of being a medical missionary to China, but then, unexpectedly, we found ourselves serving with Lutheran World Relief in Vietnam during the war in the mid-1960s. Most of my career, however, was dedicated to Latin America, where we lived for more than a dozen years serving Lutheran organizations and where I traveled extensively for another dozen for Heifer International. In the 1990s, I delved into the unknown of Central and Eastern Europe and made trips to Asia and Africa. After I retired from Heifer International in 2000, I reconnected with Central America and worked with Agros International as an advisor and trainer for another seven years.

Once I made a list of all the countries I have traveled to, and it numbered over 75. We lived in nine different countries, and Judy and I have occupied about 20 houses since we got married in 1965. Trips for work and pleasure would be in the hundreds. During an eight-year period when I was making six or seven international trips a year, I kept a log of the number of nights slept in beds other than my own at home, and I found I had been absent from my wife and family for a total of two-and-a-half years. If I had made a plan for my life while in college, it certainly would not have looked like this!

My quest and interest in the wider world was not purely spiritual. It was driven also by the appeal and adventure of travel, curiosity and the search for an interesting and relevant career. But the fact that I was drawn into a lifework involving missions and international development in developing countries was not by accident. It was based on a firm foundation in a Christian family and the Lutheran Church, plus a faith that was passed down to me by my ancestors.

A life of travel brought me into contact with the great issues and challenges of our time: hunger and poverty; war, revolutions, droughts and famine; earthquakes and hurricanes; and the reality of the oppression of the poor and the unjust systems under which they live. Travel and work also brought me face to face with the great beauty of creation—tropical beaches and sea-life under the surface of the water, majestic mountain ranges, forests, jungles, deserts, valleys and high plateaus.

Work that entails travel can stimulate the mind and inspire the soul. It can also be exhausting, draining the body of vigor. However, travel to poor communities and work with the people who live there restored me in mind and spirit again and again. I was fortunate to see many hopeful and exciting endeavors of people living

3

in poverty as they worked toward a better life in the face of extraordinary odds. I also experienced failures and times of disappointment and discouragement about the human condition and our attempts to bring hope and change.

Travel brought me to lonely places and times when I questioned whether what I was doing made a difference in the face of such huge obstacles and needs. Coming face to face with people living in impoverishing conditions, I was drawn deeper into a conviction that the great hunger of people is more than physical, social and mental progress, though it is all of these. Indeed, people in many cultural and social situations hunger for and value a deep spiritual life. I was renewed and invigorated through my sojourn among them for forty years.

Reflection

Though this is a book about my journey, I fervently hope that the contents will stimulate earnest and helpful reflections about your life experiences and spiritual journeys. If these 35 essays aid you in your discernment and provide a framework that helps you think about your own spiritual life, my purpose will have been fulfilled.

Lutheran theologian Bradley Hanson wrote, "All of us are on a spiritual journey. As spiritual beings, we are able to transcend our immediate circumstances and ask whether there is a greater reality and a larger meaning to which we may appropriately give ourselves. All of us end up answering this question by the actual course of our lives, for our daily choices reflect what is the greatest reality for us" (*A Graceful Life: Lutheran Spirituality for Today*, p. 1).

Meditation

*Surely goodness and mercy shall follow me all the days of my life,
and I shall dwell in the house of the Lord my whole life long.*

Psalm 23:6

☞ Reflect on your own journey through life.
How has your journey ebbed and flowed throughout your life?
Write about or draw a graphic representation of your life
and how God has interrupted it at certain points.

☞ What do you notice about the shape of your life?
Its turning points? Its direction?

A Spirituality of Service

*A body dies when it is separated from the spirit, and in the same way
faith is dead if it is separated from good deeds.*

James 2:26

AN IMPORTANT INTERFACE between spirituality and action may not be readily appreciated by some practitioners of Christian service. Much of the modern emphasis on spirituality is focused on the inward journey, contemplation and a growing intimacy with God. The emphasis of activists in areas of social service, justice, poverty, development and the environment has been on programs of direct service, outreach, organization and advocacy. Both are valid, and each strengthens the other. Integration brings strength. But what may not always be clear to those working in fields of social action and service is how the deepening of one's spiritual life helps to strengthen and sustain a life of service. This is especially so in the face of the challenges presented by the often overwhelming needs and demands of this calling.

One of the organizations I worked with identified spirituality as one of the cornerstones, or foundations, of its program. Yet my colleagues and I sometimes had difficulty defining what that meant, and we tended to avoid working with the concept of spirituality since it seemed vague and not easy to incorporate into the practicalities of program planning and work with communities. Nevertheless, it was taken as truth that every person has within themselves a spiritual element—albeit difficult to define. As I explored further, I began to notice that opinions like the following have become quite commonplace: "I am spiritual, but not religious," or "I don't believe in organized religion" and "She is not religious, but very spiritual."

This caused me to wonder what spirituality means. What is it? Does spirituality have relevance to life in the secular world, the world of everyday human activity and need? My view is that it does and that a spiritual life requires a degree of intentionality as we respond to God's Spirit.

I realized I needed to define spirituality for myself and find ways to be more disciplined in my own practices. I began to be mindful of God in the ordinary events of daily life, especially as I traveled to carry out my work in human development. I accumulated books, attended retreats, talked to pastors and soul mates and found a spiritual director. Later I decided to undertake training to become a spiritual director myself.

I found Presbyterian writer Marjorie Thompson's definition of the spiritual life to be straightforward and helpful. This was a good starting point for me. She says, "In one sense spirituality is simply the capacity for a spiritual life—the universal human capacity to receive, reflect and respond to the Spirit of God…. Scripturally speaking, the spiritual life is simply the increasing vitality and sway of God's Spirit in us" (*Soul Feast*, pp. 6, 7). The term sway connotes the notion of leaning into something; maybe as Thomas More so ably expressed it "to lean into the comfort of God." I have not grasped spirituality fully, yet I continue to lean into, learn and practice it in daily life.

One way to define spirituality is to see it as the pattern in which we order our lives in response to our experience of the Spirit of God; others say it is simply having an open heart and being mindful. Descriptions such as these can help us characterize a kind of universal definition of spirituality. As I looked at some of the definitions of spirituality put forth by various writers and teachers, I found myself stretching to grasp the meaning and depth of the definitions. I searched for a simple explanation that I could easily remember and visualize, perhaps one with few words. Personally, and at the risk of sounding overly pious, my image of spirituality is simply following in the footsteps of Jesus and serving others.

In 1 Peter 2:21 we read an exhortation of Peter: *For to this you have been called, because Christ also suffered for you, leaving you an example, so that you should follow in his steps.* Peter is actually writing this to slaves to help them endure unjust suffering. I am sure no Christian today would condone slavery, but we do know that many in the world today live under systems of unjust authority and lack of opportunity. I believe it is our call, as an expression of our spiritual service, to stand with the oppressed and downtrodden in the work of service, whether that means binding up their wounds, being a presence in the midst of disasters, supporting long-term development or advocating for peace and justice.

Even though I have tried to grow in faith over the years, there is a sense in which I find myself going back to the basics time and again. As I read through one note-book from long ago I was chagrined to see that I was dealing with some of the same questions and struggles that I find in journal entries years later. But I did see in this record that travel, relationships, books, worship, time in nature, work and encounters with people in my own and other cultures have kept me alive spiritually and involved emotionally and mentally for my entire adult life.

We all take different journeys in life, and some of them even entail travel. The most important journey anyone takes is the spiritual one. That journey is both external and internal, and for either of these, it is not necessary to get on an airplane or take a long road trip. In fact, one of the most challenging parts of my spiritual journey has been to make my way through the cultural changes that have taken place in the U.S. over the course of my lifetime. It has also been a challenge, at times, to avoid pessimism in the face of overwhelming needs and poverty in the many countries where I carried out my work.

Societal, cultural and technological changes have tremendously impacted the church I love, the communities where we have lived and, of course, my own fam-ily. The traditional values that underpinned my views of marriage and family have undergone dramatic change, and the exodus from the church of the generation that succeeded my own baffles my mind. In these areas I have had to grow and reflect on the meaning of all these changes.

My career in international development provided me with many opportunities and challenges. Looking back, I often felt I had the best job in the world, and I would recommend a career in international development to young people. But it does take preparation vocationally and spiritually. I am very thankful that I met and worked with people who had a similar drive to live out their faith in action for the needs of the world.

While practicing a spirituality that leads to action for the sake of the world, I need to be alert to notice the signs of God's prompting in my life; watching for the leading of the Spirit. It is all too easy to become distracted and not see the opportunities for service that present themselves. Other terms I explore in this book to help you recognize God's leading and will are discernment, waiting, listening, and responding to a call, all of which imply an attitude of attention and watchfulness.

Reflection

Phillip Britts, a British poet and horticulturist, said something in a talk during Advent in 1949 that helps make sense of how the spiritual life unfolds and why:

> We are human and finite, and thus cannot live perpetually in a sense of expectation . . . We are distracted by many things. Our spiritual awareness waxes and wanes in intensity. When we experience God's love, we turn away from the notion that we, by our religious efforts, can set something in motion that God must obey in response . . . This is why we do not come to God by musing or by contemplating our highest ideals in splendid spiritual isolation, nor by disputing religious points and striving for a state of spiritual perfection . . . Human love (as contrasted to God's love) depends on human character and certain virtuous qualities. A spiritual hierarchy is thus created in which each person climbs to a different height of godliness or saintliness according to his or her spiritual capacity. But, spiritual depth is the working of God coming down and penetrating to the depths of our hearts, and not our own soul's climbing. No ladder of mysticism can ever meet or find or possess God. Faith is the power given to us (*Watch for the Light: Readings for Advent and Christmas*, p.115).

Meditation

*Do you not know that you are God's temple,
and that God's Spirit dwells in you?*

I Corinthians 3:16

☞ Take a few minutes to think about what spirituality means to you. Write a short definition that is clear, concise and pragmatic. It may be interesting for you to come back to this definition after you have read this entire book to notice then what you have gained through your reading and reflection.

☞ Spirituality of service combines the interaction of three dynamics—mind, heart and hands. Our intellectual understanding of God is coupled with our heartfelt acceptance of that relationship and our desire to serve. How do you move your thinking about God from your head to your heart and into action?

☞ What is your spiritual tradition? What struggles have you experienced regarding that tradition? How have those experiences impacted your faith today?

☞ If you feel so prompted, close with a prayer seeking guidance for the deepening of your spiritual insight and ability to live a life of service.

Journaling the Journey

As long as you live, you learn. As long as you learn, you live.

Anonymous

I HAVE KEPT NOTES AND JOURNALS FOR MANY YEARS. They are stacked on my bookshelf, and I have taken them with me on each of our moves. Many of them were written during travels and sojourns in other countries and cultures. I can hardly estimate the number of trips I have taken, the numerous farms and families, villages and cities visited, the projects and workshops I have undertaken and the number of unique cultures I have been privileged to experience. It is hard to remember the names of all the people who have positively affected me through thousands of conversations, meals, retreats, meetings, speeches, field trips, visits in humble homes and discussions with colleagues.

Hundreds of mentors, colleagues, friends and villagers accompanied me on my 40-year career in international development. I have lost contact with a good many of them, but my journals remind me of their names and help me to remember their faces again. Some of the best of them have passed on: Bob Busche of Lutheran World Relief, Gordon Hatcher, a Quaker with whom I worked in Peru and Honduras, and Gustavo Parajon, a Baptist leader in Nicaragua, are three whose companionship I treasure in my heart.

As I became aware of a growing interest in spirituality and prayer in my life, I was drawn to journaling—writing down what I saw and experienced. These were not attempts at creative writing or efforts to pen profound and poetic testimonies. On the contrary, the entries in my journals are simple and straightforward descriptions of feelings and experiences that occurred in the course of encounters with the people and cultures wherever I found myself. Joseph Schmidt wrote about the value

11

of journaling, saying: "In our writing, our narcissism will surely manifest itself—as will our search for the deeper truth of our life. Writing has the power to focus and locate experiences so that they can be put into perspective within our total life and faith context" (*Praying our Experiences*, p. 40).

———>·◦·<———

The following are notes from a trip to Nepal where I reflected on life as an endless journey of exploration and learning.

Katmandu, Nepal, September, 1998

This is a country where many Westerners—tourists, mountain climbers and backpackers—come to commune with nature, ascend great mountains, encounter Eastern spirituality and learn the mystery of the OM: "the great stillness of pure being." Some of these travelers seem to be spiritual tourists, searching for something here that they don't think they can find back home. I am here with the Heifer staff to teach about grassroots program evaluation and to learn as much as I can about Nepal from them. I want to find out about the work they are doing in rural communities in this country. We will visit several projects, and we need to do a field test of our evaluation method, so on our first day we prepared a schedule for our time together.

Today we got out of the noisy and congested city for a short trip to visit a project. I was feeling claustrophobic in the urban area—knowing that some of the great mountains of the world were out there and I hadn't gotten a glimpse of them yet! They have been cloud-covered every day so far. Not far from the city we visited a village where about 20 colorfully dressed women with red dots on their foreheads showed up to meet with us. The dots, I learned, mean they are married, with a husband still living. The red dot on the hair-line indicates devotion to a Hindu god and a kind of veneration and worshipful attitude.
It was a very congenial meeting.

Across the valley, I saw a Buddhist temple and streamers, which were tied to trees, blowing high into the sky. Each cloth piece has a prayer attached, and it is believed these prayers float up to the heavens with the breeze.

12

Several days later I traveled with my host, Mahendra, and his team for six hours down the mountains to the lowlands in the south to visit another women's project called the Sagarnath Woman's Goat Project. Sagarnath is the Nepali word for Mount Everest, but we were about as far from that famous mountain as we could be and still be in Nepal. This is the tropical area near the Indian border, and it was very hot—about 35 degrees centigrade (almost 100 degrees Fahrenheit). We ended up almost on the Indian border at Janakpur, a city famous for a Hindu temple and a destination for many Indian Hindu pilgrims. I was fascinated and tried to take in what was going on in all the religious practices I observed as we visited a number of Hindu and Buddhist sites and temples here and in Katmandu. They have names I forgot as soon as I heard them.

Two things that I find interesting are that Buddhism is not considered so much a religion as a way of life—an attempt to connect all things; and Hinduism, with its plethora of gods, demigods and demons is not a religion that others can convert to—one must be born into it. Or at least this is what I was told.

After several days of project evaluations and religious site visits, we made the long trek back up the mountainous highway to the capitol city. We had asked questions, talked and pondered for days—discussing the meaning of this and that. I tried to understand and absorb as much as possible, covering a wide range of issues—projects, poverty, religion, spirituality, as well as Nepali history and culture. About five hours into the trip—while traversing a continuous repetition of hairpin curves, Vazrul, our colleague from Bangladesh, leaned forward and asked, "Mahendra, when will we finish this endless journey?" We burst into laughter at the irony of the question—a welcome comic relief for our sore bottoms, tired bodies and exhausted minds. Indeed the trip was a long one, but eventually we would arrive in the city. The quest to understand and know, however, is, indeed, endless.

⋙◆⋘

Some of the journals from my life-long journey remind me of experiences, people and readings that I had forgotten until I read about them years later.

New York City, January, 1981

I have been in meetings here with colleagues in Lutheran World Relief, and I am musing on how fortunate I feel to be on the cutting edge. I was with friends today who set me to thinking: How often do we get to feel the stimulation of discovery and the flash of relevance and revelation? It was exciting tonight to read *A Severe Mercy,* Sheldon Vanauken's account of his conversion, which includes some of his correspondence with C.S. Lewis.

I have only a vague memory of reading that book, but it brought back memories from England in 1960 when I read *Mere Christianity* by Lewis. I think that was the closest I came to what might be described as a conversion experience. Great clarity came to me about the Christian faith then! I had been a baptized Christian all my life—but after I read C.S. Lewis I knew why I was a Christian. Vanauken wrote in his book "The best argument for Christianity is Christians, their certainty, joy and completeness. But the strongest argument against Christianity is also Christians!" I hope I have been an argument for, not against.

⊰•⊱

Ordinary life is mostly what I observed on my travels and wrote about in my journal. Many times I have gone to the central plaza in Latin American towns and cities or to the town squares or parks in Europe or to a sidewalk restaurant or village center in Asia or Africa just to sit and watch people. In most of the world people come out in the late afternoon and evening to enjoy the social ambiance and atmosphere of their city or village.

L'viv, Ukraine, June, 1998

Many people were in the city square in the late afternoon, in a large park with benches and sidewalks, statues and a small pond. People of all ages promenaded on the main square. Old people played cards or chess and socialized—some in animated conversations—and others quietly shared some news of the day. Most impressive was the spontaneous singing by groups—mostly men—who belted out Ukrainian melodies from their religious and folk heritage, singing them from memory. There was no hurry or bustle here. Many people were just strolling and walking around—not going anywhere in particular, it would seem. Maybe it is as an Orthodox bishop from Bulgaria said when asked, "What is the difference between these streets and ours in America?" He answered, "Maybe it is because we have already arrived where we're going."

Reflection

Martin Luther's commentary on the parable of the leaven sounds surprisingly relevant to our modern ears. It is appropriate for our consideration of the life-long spiritual journey. Leaven, of course, refers to the yeast that when mixed into bread dough causes it to rise.

> The . . . parable . . . tells of the leaven which the woman mixes in three measures of meal until it is thoroughly leavened. The new leaven is the faith and grace of the Spirit. It does not leaven the whole lump at once but gently, and gradually we become like this new leaven and eventually, a bread of God. This life, therefore, is not righteousness, but growth in righteousness; not health, but healing; not being, but becoming; not rest, but exercise. We are not yet what we shall be, but we are growing toward it. The process is not yet finished, but it is going on. This is not the end, but it is the road. All does not yet gleam in glory, but all is being purified.

Meditation

I do not consider that I have made it on my own; but this one thing I do, forgetting what lies behind and straining forward to what lies ahead, I press on toward the goal for the prize of the heavenly call of God in Christ Jesus.

Philippians 3:13,14

☞ Recall a travel experience that had an important impact on you. Reflect on the people you encountered. Notice how the places and people affected you. How have these experiences impacted your faith and your spiritual life?

⌒ Think of a gift or opportunity you have been given to serve God's purposes in this world. Write about or sketch your insights, and if you are in a group, share with others.

⌒ Whether or not you are accustomed to journaling, take some time to write now. Simply write about what happened today. What feelings and emotions did you experience, and what thoughts of God or prayers to God rise up in your heart as you write about this?

Perseverance

Indeed we call blessed those who showed endurance.

James 5:11

Holy Trinity Center, near Baltimore, May 9, 2001

I am here for the second annual residency retreat of the group spiritual direction study program, and I am in a bit of pain. On our farm a few days ago, our young horse Jake got out of control and galloped across the fields and out of sight. After several days of searching, we finally located him at a neighbor's farm a few miles distant, and I went to retrieve him. Because he was rather agitated, I decided it would be best to walk him the several miles back to our farm. That worked for a while, but about a mile from home, Jake was spooked by a flock of passing geese and bolted to the right, catching me broadside with the full force of his body on my side. As a result I feel lots of pain when I twist, stretch, cough or laugh. I may have bruised or cracked ribs—Ouch!

Let me explain how this incident with my horse Jake and a recent trip to Guatemala taught me something about perseverance.

A few weeks ago I had a mountaintop experience at Lake Atitlan in Guatemala (described in the chapter on Contemplation). That was quickly followed by coming down the mountain to be in the midst of the poverty and struggle for survival of rural Indian families I work with through the Agros program in Guatemala. The families who participate in the program were harshly and unjustly repressed during the long civil war in Guatemala in the 1970s and '80s. Many families lost everything—family members were killed, homes burned and villages razed. Whole communities fled into the mountains and forests, spending months and years as refugees in the rugged terrain of northern Guatemala or

17

across the border in Mexico. For almost 15 years, Agros has worked with these people to restore hope; helping many Indian families rebuild their lives and communities. I am reminded of a homecoming from another exile, when the people of Israel returned from captivity. The writer of Psalm 126 encourages the people; even though they are weary, they will reap a harvest of joy: *May those who sow in tears reap with shouts of joy! Those who go out weeping, bearing the seed for sowing, shall come home with shouts of joy, carrying their sheaves* (Psalm 126:5, 6).

I feel fortunate to have a part in this program. Agros is a Christian-inspired organization supported and staffed by people who take both action and prayer seriously. We are frequently requested to pray for specific communities, families or situations. I confess that I am not totally reliable in remembering to make continuous intercession. I wonder about my own level of commitment to prayer that perseveres in supplications for all the saints, since I so easily wander off the path.

This morning at the retreat center an analogy occurred to me. I began comparing my own minor discomfort of aches and pains to the major challenges faced by the Indian families we accompany in the Ixil area of Guatemala. Because of my temporary injury I am having difficulty sleeping through the night and getting out of bed in the morning. When I awaken during the night or early morning, the first and only thing on my mind is how to get out of bed with the least amount of pain possible. My focus is on my immediate need and my concern is to get up and get going. I find that certain movements will cause pain, so I try to avoid these as much as possible. Sometimes I feel doubtful that prayer will fix this problem, but I have hope and expect that this will pass and I will be "whole" again. Healing will come in due time and I patiently wait for it.

Similarly, the poor have their daily struggles and the challenge of getting up and making it through each day. They are anxious about putting food on the table and concerned about earning a bit of money or worried about a sick or hungry child. These are the daily struggles of many people in Central America. Because of the past injustices these indigenous people have suffered, Agros prioritizes work with this population. The poor live with relentless demands and a less than optimistic prospect for improvement. While praying for God's help they live an exhausting life—working, walking, worrying and wondering where they will obtain their daily bread.

Will my intercessory prayers help these Ixiles with their challenges and problems? In worship services we often pray for "the poor, the hungry, and those suffering in mind, body and spirit." This is an important, though somewhat generalized, supplication. Ideally the people of God should get involved and do something specific for a community, even though it is not realistic to expect all members of a church to have direct encounters with the poor. But there are ways to form relationships with communities and churches in countries like Guatemala, and most denominations and organizations like Agros have structured opportunities for such action.

We do have the promise of the Gospel and the hope of the ages from Scripture—many examples of faithful prayers for the poor and disconsolate. Often I become aware of or know people in pain and nearing death for whom we are asked to pray. I need to remind myself that Jesus himself told us to put all needs before God the Father in heaven.

Over the years between 2000 and 2008, I made numerous trips back to Central America to train and advise the Agros teams in that region. In a real sense this was a spiritual journey greatly enriched by my encounter with the indigenous people who had suffered some of the worst injustices imposed on any people in the hemisphere over the last 40 years. In the past—back in the 70s and 80s—Judy and I tried to be open to the call of God through programs and organizations of the churches, making ourselves available to respond to real needs and challenges. We spent over five years in Central America; living in Nicaragua, Honduras and Guatemala. Now I had the privilege of a re-encounter with the incredibly hospitable people of Central America, trying to integrate a more mature and holistic understanding to the challenges of poverty, human rights and development.

In a recent workshop I felt humbled as I listened to the stories of people who were severely persecuted in the 70s and 80s—people who lost everything but their faith. When I travel back to Guatemala now, there is relative peace in the countryside. But the poor are still poor and I reflect on these questions: What did all the bloodshed and struggle gain? Who paid the price?

19

One morning in Guatemala, my devotional reading was about the miracle of the big catch of fish and Peter leaving everything and following Jesus. Think of how half-hearted and off the path the disciples became at times and how Peter denied Jesus. The same happens to me. I stumble along at times half-heartedly believing that I can do much in this world of such overwhelming need. I question if I can make a difference.

That morning I went into a local church to attend mass—a very full liturgy in a side chapel. Many were there even though it was a weekday. There was a mixed group of worshippers—very humble indigenous people together with better-dressed members of the middle class. They were faithful followers of the way. They knew the liturgical responses by heart and prayed with obvious fervor. They were there to hear the good news and to receive sustenance for their personal journeys. I have heard some of their stories: the yokes they have to bear and the poverty in which they live. I cannot walk in their shoes, but I have a feeling that whatever their stories, they were staying with the journey, and that encourages me to do the same.

Reflection

Endurance, perseverance and fortitude are valuable qualities for people who undergo suffering. Many have endured the pain of loss, death and injustice and make the choice to reject God's compassion. Others choose the discipline of patience and receive much comfort from the Spirit during times of suffering. This is beautifully expressed by James when he says . . . *Remember it is those who had endurance that we say are the blessed ones* (James 5:11). I have often wondered why some stay close to God or even grow in faith through times of trial while others take the path of despair and desolation.

Meditation

*Pray in the Spirit at all times . . . To that end keep alert
and always persevere in supplications for all the saints.*

Ephesians 6:18

☞ Standing alongside someone in need can help that person (or group) come out better on the other side of a difficult situation. Think of a time when your perseverance on behalf of another led to a positive outcome.

☞ Many people struggle with the issue of justice. How do you respond to those who reject or blame God in the face of injustice and suffering?

☞ Who or what in your life encourages you and gives you renewed determination to persevere in spite of setbacks and loss?

☞ To whom do you reach out when you have suffered loss or become spiritually depleted? In those times what have these people offered that has been most helpful to you?

PART TWO

Spiritual Practices

ALL RELIGIONS OFFER DISCIPLINES and practices for communicating with God; or perhaps better said, for opening oneself to a relationship and union with the Divine Presence. Christians find many references and examples in the Scriptures regarding prayer, worship, fasting and discernment. In recent years, there has been a resurgence of interest in meditation on the Word and a rediscovery of the value of silence and contemplative prayer.

Parker Palmer suggests that the term "inner work" . . .

> should become commonplace in families, schools and
> religious institutions, at least, helping us understand that
> inner work is as real as outer work and involves skills
> one can develop and use such as journaling, reflective
> reading, spiritual friendship, meditation and prayer
> (*Let Your Life Speak*, p. 91).

The following section shows how practices and disciplines can be interwoven with and become an integral part of the ebb and flow of life and work in the world. While this is not intended as a primer on particular prayer practices, I have attempted to clarify some of the terms and briefly describe how I came to understand and use these practices in my life.

Discernment

Prayer is the starting place of discernment
as well as the atmosphere in which it takes place.

Rose Mary Dougherty

Minneapolis, Minnesota, *December 23, 1972*

Our family has been back from Peru for almost a month, and we are trying to deal with how different this city is from our tropical jungle habitat of the last several years. Judy and I have experienced both reverse culture shock and some degree of anxiety. We are uncertain about our future. We have been thinking and talking about this and privately praying for some clarity.

As we drove home from a Christmas shopping outing to our temporary quarters in an upstairs apartment on Chicago Avenue, we listened to the evening news. Suddenly there was an announcement of a massive earthquake in Managua, Nicaragua. Our ears perked up as we heard about the magnitude of the quake, the initial report of numbers killed and displaced and the fires that had been ignited in the city. We cast knowing glances at each other. Though we didn't say anything, we both intuitively knew that this was news of our future. This is where we were going next.

———◆———

Ever since we decided some months earlier that it was time to leave Peru and make ourselves available for another assignment with the church, we had been talking and thinking about our future. We indicated to the mission board that we were open and interested in continuing in some kind of work overseas. But there had not been any concrete offers or openings. It was not at all clear what our future would hold and what we would do next. Response to humanitarian emergencies had been a part of our experience previously, both in Peru and Vietnam, with Lutheran World Relief. In 1966 we went to Vietnam when we were asked to be a part of the Christian presence in the midst of the human suffering that was caused by the conflagration of the war. We immersed ourselves in that work for two years, a truly life changing experience.

In 1970, just one month after we arrived in Peru, a huge earthquake rocked a large area of the coast and sierra of northern Peru. I was immediately drawn into the response to that disaster and lived for many months in a tent behind the hospital in Huarmey—the only building still standing in that coastal city. From there, I directed the work of Church World Service (CWS) in about a hundred villages in the Andean mountains. I was not qualified for, nor experienced in, that kind of disaster response. When we went to Peru, we had no inkling that disaster response and a rebuilding program would be my job; it just happened that way. Looking back, all I can say about it is that it seemed to be "the right thing to do," and I was available at the right time.

Now we found ourselves in a similar situation, perhaps the right people available at the right time and place. A month before we left Peru, we received a visit from Dwight Schwartzendruber (we called him Swartz), the Director for Programs in Latin America for Church World Service. He had come to see our small project in the jungle, which was partially funded by CWS. I had a gut feeling I would be hearing from and seeing him again. Now back in my parents' home in Minnesota, just two days after the Christmas Eve earthquake in Managua, we received a call from Church World Service in New York. Swartz asked if I would consider going immediately to Managua to organize the relief response of CWS and Lutheran World Relief. Within a week, I was on the ground in Managua, the beginning of one of the biggest and most meaningful challenges of our lives. Later Judy and the kids moved to Managua and we lived in Central America for almost six years. During that time I worked with local Protestant and Evangelical churches to help build programs and organizations that continue to the present time. These programs started with emergency relief and then matured into long-term social and human development efforts with the poor.

What does this have to do with discernment? Discernment focuses on how we make decisions, what we decide to do with our lives and for what purpose. One of the major questions faced in life is this—what should I do with this one life I have to live? For the Christian that question can be phrased as "What is God's will for my life?" Or it can be expressed as "How do I fit into God's purpose in this world?"

In practice, this big question has to be condensed to a more manageable one in time and place, such as, "Does this job opportunity fit into God's purposes and will for my life?" Though the decision may not always have to do with one's vocational choice, there are many decisions to be faced on our journey. If we are facing a major decision in life and want our answer to be in line with God's reign, then framing the right question is an important step in the process of discernment. This is what Henri Nouwen did at several critical points in his life. He took discernment very seriously, as described in the following example:

In 1981 Henri Nouwen set off on a six-month sojourn in Bolivia and Peru to discern one question: Does God call me to live and work in Latin America in the years to come? His journal of that six-month journey of discernment, eventually published in a book entitled *Gracias!*, is an intriguing story of discernment. At the end of that journey, Henri seems to have received much clarity and was near to an answer to his discernment question. He had prayed daily, talked to priests, bishops and theologians as well as laity and other professionals. He studied, read widely and keenly observed the political, social and cultural situation of Peru and Bolivia. He immersed himself with the people in a slum area around Lima and lived with a poor family.

In his last days in Peru, he writes sentences like this: "Just three days before my return to the United States, an appealing, clear, and convincing vocation has started to take form. Many things that Mattias proposed had certain obviousness to me. (Mattias was a priest working in the Cusco area whose opinion Nouwen particularly trusted). The more I thought about them during the day, the more I felt that things fit very well and that I have as much clarity and certainty as I probably will ever have." Later he wrote, "My impressions of ministry in Peru are starting to show patterns and my future plans are slowly taking some identifiable shape . . . There was a sense of harmony, of belonging, yes, maybe even of vocation. To find that vocation, I had come to Peru." He sounded almost ecstatic and certain that he had discerned the will of God for his future life and ministry in Peru (*Gracias!*—from the chapter titled "The Outline of a Vision," pp. 157–185). The sojourn in Latin America had a profound effect on Henri Nouwen. This spiritual mentor to countless thousands was a restless soul.

With apparent clarity about his future, he returned to the U.S. to talk about his discernment journey and get reactions to this proposed vocational change from trusted friends and colleagues in Holland and America. We don't know many of the details of these consultations and the mental and spiritual process he went through after he left Peru. But we do know that he never returned to Peru and that his ministry took a distinctly different direction. He ended his ministry and the last decade of his life in the Daybreak community, L'Arche, in Montreal, as a pastor and worker amongst people with severe physical and mental disabilities.

Nouwen was a man of great spiritual, mental and relational gifts, and most of his adult life he was on a journey of preparation. When I look at the example of a spiritual giant such as Henri Nouwen and see his struggles with discernment and finding the will of God for his life, I feel somewhat reassured about my own struggles and difficulty with major decisions in life. I see from this example that discernment can be a long and demanding process. What sometimes seems to be a clear answer regarding God's purposes for oneself may later take a turn that leads in unexpected directions.

Many times in my life, I have come to a crossroads and wondered about the path ahead. Judy and I took the path through our married life in relatively small chunks of two to five years at a time. That was not by plan or design—it just seemed to happen that way. At numerous points we faced major decisions about what to do, where to live and how best to serve. All the thinking and pondering was sometimes answered for us in an instant, and we would know immediately what we should do. Calls came at completely unexpected times asking us to respond to a natural disaster or a mounting humanitarian emergency: the war in Vietnam, earthquakes in Peru, Nicaragua and Guatemala, a hurricane in Honduras.

At other times we struggled with questions of major change for months, even years, before we came to our decision. We made inquiries about opportunities for jobs, places we might like to live and organizations and ministries that seemed appealing.

We would talk it through for hours and at times would tire of the continuing, nagging uncertainty about what course to take. We would say we were praying about it; but to be honest, many times I neglected to bring the question to God in prayer in a continuous way. Nevertheless, having our faith as the underpinning of our lives meant that ultimately our quest for direction came from that source, and we had to trust our intuition and reasoning abilities when we felt and agreed, "It's the right thing to do."

There are many good examples of discernment from Scripture, but there is one that grabs my attention as rather curious and strange. It comes from the Acts of the Apostles when the disciples are choosing a replacement for Judas. There are two good candidates:

So one of the men who have accompanied us during all the time the Lord Jesus went in and out among us, beginning from the baptism of John until the day when he was taken up from us—one of these must become witness with us to his resurrection. So they proposed two, Joseph called Barsabbas, who was also known as Justus, and Matthias. Then they prayed and said, "Lord, you know everyone's heart. Show us which one of these two you have chosen to take the place in this ministry and apostleship from which Judas turned aside to go to his own place." And they cast lots for them, and the lot fell on Matthias; and he was added to the eleven apostles (Acts 1: 21–26).

They cast lots? They rolled dice to make an important decision? Why? Several things are clear in this example. To start with they agreed on a guiding principle— it should be someone who "had accompanied us during all the time the Lord Jesus went in and out among us." Secondly they had two good candidates, and both options were good and acceptable. This seems to be a good process for decision-making at any time, but the difference is that "they prayed about it" and apparently felt that either choice would be good in this case. So the fair thing to do seemed to be to cast lots, and Matthias won. Well, that is the last we hear about him in Scripture, but we can assume he worked out in that job just fine—otherwise we might have heard something more.

In any or all phases of life we may be presented with discernment questions about what course to take. Concerned with how our choices fit into God's plans and purpose, at least for the major decisions, we should pray about it. That has been our experience. Many people face numerous forks in the road as they go through life, and this is not to say that a decision-making process that does not "turn to God" leads to poor decisions. But for anyone motivated to live a life in the footsteps of Jesus, discernment through prayer makes a lot of sense.

For Judy and me, sometimes the answers to our discernment questions came in the suddenness of an earthquake. At other times it was more like a full and exhaustive analysis of options—a process that included prayer and thinking about how a particular choice might fit life as we wanted to live it as Christians.

In the process of discernment, there may be many distractions clamoring for our attention. Certainly, discernment involves listening carefully to people and giving much attention to the reality of our situation, but it also means quietly listening to the movements of the Spirit through prayer.

My prayers for wisdom to make good decisions about the future have always become utterly mixed up with personal awareness—likes and dislikes, opportunities of the moment, the prospects of adventure, anxieties and the support of others. Yes, and also pride—a chance to advance in my career or impress others! But the reassurances from my wife and close friends have been among the most important factors. What mattered most is that we were true to our own values and open to where we could be of service to people in the most complete way possible—a place where we could follow the great commandment:

The first is this, *And you shall love the Lord your God with all your heart and with all your mind, and with all your strength.* The second is this, *You shall love your neighbor as yourself* (Mark 12: 30-31).

Reflection

In 2003 I had the chance to attend a spiritual retreat and listen to Nancy Reeves talk about discernment. She had written several books on the subject and pointed out three prerequisites for discernment:

> *Good relationships.* It goes without saying that one must be in a relationship with God in order to discern God's will. But it is also important to have good relationships with others, a support system, people whose opinion we trust and we can depend on.

Good self-awareness. This means, among other things, knowing myself well enough to prevent my mind from becoming cluttered with the many distractions that clamor for my attention.

Good living or "right" living. I suppose that means things like, "Love your neighbor as yourself"—and being serious about prayers like "Thy will be done;" "Forgive us our sins as we forgive those who sin against us;" and "Lead us not into temptation but deliver us from evil."

Nancy Reeves wrote this about the benefits of intentional spiritual practices for discerning God's will:

In any human endeavor preparation smoothes the path. The prerequisites for smoothing the discernment process include having an intentional spirituality with spiritual practices, combined with some degree of self-awareness and right living (*I'd Say Yes, God, If I Knew What You Wanted*, p. 29).

Meditation

And God, who searches the heart, knows what is the mind of the Spirit, because the Spirit intercedes for the saints according to the will of God. We know that all things work together for good for those who love God, who are called according to his purpose.

Romans 8:27, 28

- ☞ What process do you follow when faced with a major decision?

- ☞ Reflect on a time when you felt peace with making a major life decision. Was it an answer to prayer? Was it verbalized pleadings or just an awareness of your desire for direction?

- ☞ What persons in your life: friend, family member or helping professional, are most helpful to you in making major decisions about your direction in life?

- ☞ Currently what question of discernment are you facing?

Patience

Be still before the Lord and wait patiently for him.

Psalm 37:7

Bolivia, August 26, 1991

On a trip to visit projects of the Bolivian Lutheran Church supported by Lutheran World Relief (LWR) of Canada, we travelled out from La Paz over the vast and desolate *altiplano* (the high plateau) and down into one of the *valles* (the valleys) to a community called Moco Moco. This is the place where the first Lutheran missionaries from the World Mission Prayer League came when they arrived in Bolivia in 1938. It is the birthplace of what is now the Bolivian Lutheran Church. What isolation those missionaries lived with and what patience and fortitude they needed! In the early days of missionary work the missioners went out on five- or six-year terms of service. They had very slow and unreliable mail service for communicating with families and supporters back in their home country. Quite a contrast to our instant communications and lack of patience in today's world!

This trip took us about six hours over mostly pothole-strewn asphalt roads. We made slow progress, passing through many villages. We stopped for a break at a place in view of Lake Titicaca, the highest navigable lake in the world. I saw a sign and asked for a translation of the Quechua phrase—"My home is your home—my land is your land." I think of how this became a cruel irony and prophesy. The Spaniards came and took possession of this new world and in effect said, "Your land is my land!" The *conquistadores* not only discovered—they took possession, plundered and raped this new land. Five centuries later we see the results, and now the graffiti on many walls reads *500 Anos de Resistencia!*—500 years of resistance. That's the epitome of patience!

Moco Moco means elbow-to-elbow in the Aymara language. I did not learn the etiology of that name. Maybe people felt crowded in this valley. It is supposedly a town of over 3,000 people—though it appears larger because of its many abandoned houses, which have been left empty when people migrated to the cities in hope of a more prosperous life. An estimated 25 percent of the population keeps double residences, moving from the village to the city and back again according to seasonal agricultural cycles.

It is a pleasure to be in this indigenous community and enjoy the hospitality of the Aymara people, and I am glad to be a part of LWR's support for health and agriculture projects here. I met Manuel Loayza, one of the first Lutheran pastors in all of Bolivia. He is still working as a pastor and a leader of the potable water committee, a pillar of the community. What a privilege to meet him! His congregation is not large, about 60 members. I ask about the history of the Lutheran missions and church here in Bolivia. It was not without its conflicts and challenges. As in other Latin America countries, some of the Evangelical and Pentecostal churches seem to be in a perpetual process of splits and reconfigurations of denominations and churches.

I met Hans and Elizabeth, a German Lutheran couple serving the church as missionaries. They impressed me as coming close to living with the people, an ideal often spoken of by missionaries but not often lived out in reality. This couple is capable, motivated, energetic and sensitive. People seemed to be comfortable coming into their home, showing up for a meal, asking for advice and help with small and large problems. Theirs is the kind of presence that brings unity and healing into the community rather than division and competition.

The health project Canadian Lutheran World Relief is supporting serves several communities with a total population of about 2,500 families. With donated money for the construction of a bridge, it is possible for the health promoters to get to more villages. Through hard work and ingenuity, they have established a cold chain to keep critical medications and vaccinations cool so they can transport them to formerly isolated communities. It is always an honor to visit communities as a representative of an organization that has given much needed and appreciated help. I wish I were able to adequately interpret this experience to members in the pews of churches back in the U.S. and Canada, to let them know that their contributions do make a difference.

August 29, 1991

We left Moco Moco early in the morning, heading back to LaPaz. As usual in these small towns, people asked to catch a ride, so we took as many as we could get in the car. About an hour up the road, we came to a landslide where numerous vehicles were blocked from going forward until a mass of rocks and dirt was cleared. Two trucks full of cargo and passengers had been waiting there since last night. Luckily our wait was shorter since we arrived just as the *tractorista* (the bulldozer operator) and his machine pulled in.

This roadblock gave me time to sit in the sun on the side of a slope in those rugged and high Andean mountains and write, think and reflect. I have noticed how I've had to slow down the clock this week. Things just go slower here. For people in this culture, waiting is taken in stride—nobody gets upset or excited. We had many hours of travel ahead of us to reach La Paz, and I was on a schedule. I needed to be there for a meeting in the afternoon. But this roadblock changed all that. I was forced to change my impatient mentality with enforced waiting. What else could I do? The clearing of the road was in other hands. There was little to be gained in becoming anxious.

I wondered about the future for the people here amidst so much poverty and such scarce resources, worn-out land, few government services and little money. I thought about the people I had just left behind in Moco Moco. Are they not the least of these that Jesus talked about?

I heard the sound of the Caterpillar around the corner. Hopefully our rescue was at hand. But it was quiet where I sat. Hundreds of feet below I heard the rush of the river. Maybe I need more roadblocks in my life—intentional times for slowing down and forgetting schedules and to-do lists. I slowly repeated the verse from Psalm 46: *Be still and know that I am God.*

I noticed the sounds—the river in the distant canyon, the birds of the Andes, the bulldozer in the distance, the Aymaras quietly conversing and laughing. *Campesinos* (peasants) walked by and gave a greeting; condors glided noiselessly through the valley, and I felt the breeze through my hair. I said a silent prayer, "Lord, give me a roadblock once in awhile," and I gave thanks for this impediment in the road. Without it, I would not have noticed this beauty and peacefulness. I would have been on the road, bouncing around in the vehicle and looking out the window as we traversed the *altiplano*.

September 2, 1991

I did make it back to La Paz but not to my scheduled meeting. From there I continued on my trip to the lowlands of Bolivia and later back to the *altiplano* again, taking a bus overland from La Paz to Puno, Peru, an eight-hour trip. I was not overly anxious for it to end. On this trip I visited several projects and met many people. I saw only small improvements in the lives of the poor through the efforts of these projects, though occasionally there were dramatic transformations—only occasionally. All of these people and their organizations are working at the process of human development. It is a process that takes much patience and perseverance. From long experience, I know that among the most important principles of effective development programs are staying power, sticking with the people, and patience!

As I kept moving through this long journey, I was transfixed by the geography of the high plateaus of Peru and Bolivia. I observed the natural features and the lives of humans and animals as we sped along Lake Titicaca, hour after hour. I thought of adjectives—drab, stark, rugged, rustic, inhospitable. But I also sensed the beauty and splendor here, and I knew that this unique part of the world could teach me about hospitality, patience and appreciation for the life and culture of an ancient people.

Reflection

I know in my heart that patience involves appreciating what presents itself in the here and now. Impatience has to do with anxiety about time and the desire to escape from the here and now.

In writing about the slower pace he found in the monastery where he spent some months, Henri Nouwen offered this anecdote:

> I am beginning to discover the "other world" in which I live. When I run, monks smile; when I work very intensely, they make signs to slow

down; and when I worry, I know it is usually useless. Last week I asked John Eudes how he thought I was doing. He said, "I guess OK. Nobody has mentioned you yet." That would not be a good sign everywhere! I really must enter that "other side," the quiet, rhythmic, solid side of life, the deep solid stream moving underneath the restless waves of my sea (*The Genesee Dairy: Report from a Trappist Monastery* p. 37).

Meditation

May you be made strong with all the strength that comes from his glorious power, and may you be prepared to endure everything with patience, while joyfully giving thanks to the Father who has enabled you to share in the inheritance of the saints in the light.

Colossians 1:11–12

☞ Reflect on an experience that forced you to completely change your plans and literally helped you slow down and consider more important things.

☞ What is your general pattern for dealing with a situation where you are forced to wait? What do you learn about yourself from this?

☞ Is there something in your life these days that you must endure with patience?

☞ How can you intentionally practice patience by setting aside time and space for quietude, meditation and appreciation of your surroundings?

Self-Examination

Self-examination is not morbid introspection or self-condemnation,
but the honest, fearless confrontation of the self,
and its abandonment to God in trust.

Kenneth Leach, Anglican priest

SELF-EXAMINATION LEADS TO SELF-KNOWLEDGE. Journaling is one way I use to give myself feedback and carry on an internal dialogue. Here is what I wrote over a period of some days in 1997.

Little Rock, Arkansas, *August, 1997*

It was an average week at work (not traveling at this time). I can't recall anything particularly memorable, the same for my noticing of God in my life. At church on Sunday, I didn't get much from the sermon entitled "Come and See." At the council meeting on Sunday night, I participated pretty well—the usual issues and discussion of a small and struggling church. On Monday, we served a meal at the homeless shelter, Our House. I felt good about doing this. There were more people to serve than we had planned for, so it was a bit of a hassle. It was wonderful to watch our six-year old-granddaughter Leslie who was with us interact so spontaneously with homeless people.

The next day Leslie and I went out to the parking lot where she rode her bike on her own. I saw the wonder in her eyes as she felt the sensation of riding without help for the first time. I felt great satisfaction. There are just a few things in life that one remembers doing for the very first time.

Our recent vacation was quite active—the nature of vacations—to give us a change of pace. I wanted the vacation to be more than a rushed trip out West or an attempt to get to as many sites as possible in the time available. I have noticed that for me, this vacation did not lend itself to reading, daily prayer, and staying current with the news. But it did offer a change of scenery, time to talk things through with Judy, an opportunity for seeing family, as well as contemplating and appreciating the natural world, and quiet moments for dreaming and thinking about the future. We also visited different churches for a variety of worship experiences. I have noticed lately that my prayers are less verbal as I sit in wonder and in the presence of the created order. Words pass away and are replaced by simply being still, open and listening, looking up unto the hills—living in the present.

———◆◆◇———

It can be readily seen that the above paragraphs are not steeped in insight or great wisdom. These are simply ruminations on what was happening in my life over a short period of time and indications of my feelings and thoughts about these occurrences. Many times when I sit down to write in my journal, I feel as if there is absolutely nothing of significance to write. Life has just been ordinary. But as I write, I think of what has happened and in jotting down these short descriptions, my pen prompts me to remember other related thoughts, feelings and even prayers of petition and gratitude. Journaling seems to gift one with the opportunity to express the sacred in the ordinary.

It is difficult to evaluate one's own life and easy to become frustrated at the insufficient depth and attention given to the spiritual life. People tend to be rather self-critical when considering their spiritual and prayer practices. When I measure myself by the high standards of spiritual heroes in my life or by lofty pronouncements of preachers or many writers of books on spirituality, I feel that I have accomplished little. But then I find that even the most saintly people I have encountered will often castigate themselves and express dissatisfaction for their lack of consistency in prayer.

For some, the notion of regular prayer may not even cross their minds, and on the surface at least, they seem to go through life ignoring the promptings of the Spirit. My opinion is that the Spirit of God is within all humans, but each person has the freedom of choice—to ignore or respond to that presence. When I hear someone criticizing the behaviors and actions of others, I wonder if they are looking self-critically at their own life—"Those hypocrites who call themselves Christians!" they say. Judgment of others is a temptation for Christians and non-Christians alike.

It is also difficult to evaluate our own spiritual journey, especially if we are thinking of it as a movement toward achievement of goals, a process that results in perfection. Henri Nouwen wrote, "Those who think they have arrived have lost their way. Those who think they have reached their goal have missed it" (*The Genesee Diary*, p.133). It occurs to me that my own approach to self-examination may be flawed if I only use external markers as measures of living up to my ideals and values.

I look at the ideals set forth in Scripture—the fruits of the Spirit, for example, or the practices of the great spiritual giants of the centuries, such as John of the Cross. The problem is that I may be searching and studying with my head more than with my heart. Growth in the spiritual life depends on both an honest inquiry of external behavior and an examination of the inner life.

In my work as a trainer I observe that there are few who really ask for and are ready to receive feedback. I suspect this is because they fear criticism. But listening to feedback is essential for personal growth. The same applies to feedback from others on our spiritual lives. I have come to believe that it is next to impossible to be a totally private Christian. I need the support, feedback and accountability of being a part of the Body of Christ.

Spiritual directors generally do not give advice, but one of the best pieces of advice I ever got was from Sister Martha Ann, my spiritual director. Once when I was lamenting my poor prayer life, she said, "Why are you so hard on yourself? Remember to pray as you can, not as you can't." This is not an original thought from her, but it was spoken to me at the right moment, and it has stuck with me. She also humorously told me of a pastor who was in spiritual direction with her. When she asked for feedback about how the process was going for him, he said, "Well, you could kick butt a little more!"

Perhaps kicking butt has been used for too long in the Church. I am quite certain that criticism and badgering people from the pulpit is not helpful. Being in an honest and loving relationship with a soul mate can be very valuable, even if it sometimes means administering hard love. I find that I need to be reminded to notice the ways that God is answering prayer. Sometimes I notice it by myself, but at other times a reminder comes from unexpected sources.

Sister Martha Ann also recommended that I practice examination of consciousness, not of conscience. This means a simple scanning of the conscious mind to recall what has happened during the day and to review behaviors, thoughts and attitudes of that day. Sometimes events which seem like faults and dissonance can prompt us to prayers of confession and repentance, leading to forgiveness. That which gives us consonance, a sense of rightness, leads us into the loving presence of the Lord and God's Grace. There are even times when we revel in the moment so much that we can say to ourselves "It doesn't get any better than this!"

Reflection

Marjorie Thompson offers a helpful explanation of the practice of Examen outlined by Saint Ignatius (the founder of the Jesuit Order):

> In historical terms, "examination of conscience" has often included awareness of the graced moments of our lives along with our miserable failings. The practice of Examen . . . includes discerning consolations and desolations. Consolation refers to that state in which we experience the presence and grace of God, and it calls for gratitude. Desolation represents the opposite state, and it calls for confession (*Soul Feast: an Invitation to the Christian Spiritual Life*, p. 100).

Meditation

Search me, O God, and know my heart; test me and know my thoughts.
Psalm 139:23

☞ Close your eyes and take five minutes to mentally scan through this day. What feelings and images arise in your heart and mind?

☞ When you reviewed your day (or week), what elements drew you toward God and gave you a sense of peace? Which recollections bring about feelings of anxiety and stress?

☞ What specifically are those things in your life that distract you from your spiritual center?

☞ How does your spiritual life vary when you are on vacation, at work, in Church, out in nature or with family? Are there any patterns you wish to change?

Conversation

When you speak to me about your deepest questions,
you do not want to be fixed or saved; you want to be seen and heard,
to have your truth acknowledged and honored.

Parker Palmer, A Hidden Wholeness, p. 117

Tegucigalpa, Honduras, *February, 1997*

I am back in Honduras after almost eleven years. Central America is a place from my past with which I have had little connection in recent years. Tim Wheeler picked me up at the airport. He has the same shy grin I remember from back when I first met him over twenty years ago. In 1976 we both came to Honduras after *Fifi*, the hurricane that wreaked havoc and did so much destruction in the northern part of the country. Our family was living in Nicaragua at that time, serving Lutheran World Relief, and I traveled here often to work in the relief response to that natural and humanitarian disaster. In early 1978, we moved here to work with an organization of the Evangelical churches of Honduras. That was during the decade when I seemed to be going from disaster to disaster every two years: Peru, Nicaragua, Honduras, Guatemala, El Salvador.

Tim met Gloria soon after he arrived in Honduras, and they fell madly in love. He is totally devoted to her and still beams like a little boy and shows the love he has for her in the most charming ways. He seems to feel amazed at how lucky he is that she loves him and that they got married.

We left Honduras after their wedding in July of 1978, even though we were invited to stay and keep working here. There was much to do, and we have reflected often on how different our lives would have been if we had taken that path. Isn't that true of so many major decisions in life—thinking about "what if"?

41

I am staying at Tim and Gloria's home. During supper we talked of many things we have in common and memories of the long ago. It is easy to engage in conversation with friends with whom we have shared meaningful experiences in the past. Sometimes silence comes in short and quiet interludes during the conversation.

I asked Gloria about her mother's death, and she related the story with some difficulty. She feels guilty about how it happened. She took her mother with her on a trip to a remote village some three hours off the main road. Her mother suffered a heart attack or stroke—not sure which—and had to be brought a long distance, first by stretcher and then to a hospital in a pickup. She never regained consciousness and died two days later in the hospital. Gloria was not comfortable with face-to-face conversation, at least not this conversation. She told the story with tears in her eyes, without making eye contact. Tim and I sat quietly listening, not interrupting. We allowed pauses of silence during the conversation and we were comfortable with that. We were talking in English mixed with Spanish. It was a personally satisfying time—being with friends and sharing conversation.

<hr />

Conversation can be a spiritual practice, but not all conversation is—nor should it be. Cocktail party banter is not; discussing and debating issues is not; and most coffee-hour fellowship time after worship is not. That doesn't mean this kind of interpersonal communication or small talk is a waste of time, but sometimes it feels like it.

Uninterrupted listening is an important skill for friends and especially for spiritual companions. In fact, listening is important for anyone who wants to be helpful to others. My friend Susan is good at the kind of conversation that goes deeper. She asks good questions and has a way of going to *al grano* (to the point) as is said in Spanish. Some people have the knack for listening and not disturbing the quiet interludes. I have been in many conversations that bounce from one topic to another, and I find myself thinking, "Why are we talking about this?"

Writers on the topic of interpersonal communication often stress the importance of careful listening. After all, a good conversation should be proportionately speaking

42

and listening. But many of us, because of our anxiety and discomfort with silent pauses, may jump too quickly to tell our own story or strive to say something immediately helpful. We fail to recognize the value of listening, in and of itself.

There were many opportunities for conversation on this trip. Some days later I stayed in Monte Carmelo, a training and conference center where many workshops are held and where North American church people come to stay for part of their time when on study trips. A group of Presbyterians was here analyzing the realities of life in Honduras. I tried to engage in conversation, but several of them talked a lot and seemed to think they actually understood *la realidad* (the reality). I became irritated and retreated to my room.

Later I talked for several hours with a Presbyterian missionary who had been in Central America continuously for decades. He had more reason to know *la realidad* than I did, for sure. I felt discouraged after our conversation. He told me much about conflicts in the churches, group in-fighting, rightists versus leftists and power struggles. Later, in my prayers, I wondered how Jesus feels about followers who drift far from the spiritual basis and the grounding they were given by His teachings and example. It is good to have this conversation with the Lord—though it is perhaps a bit one-sided, that is to say, my side. I took some time for silence, reflection and writing, a welcome relief from too many spoken words.

I awoke after a restful night. It is good to awaken in these sparse surroundings. The cool quiet of Monte Carmelo this morning quickened my senses. I heard birds singing and the background of distant traffic—noise that did not distract from my inner calm. It felt good to be here—good to sit in quiet contemplation for about 20 minutes before I let the coming events of the day invade my mind and overtake the inner and outer silence. I was ready for another day filled with small talk, discussion and, I hope, some good conversation and listening.

Reflection

Dietrich Bonhoeffer wrote about the ministry of listening as a Christian service:

> Many people are looking for an ear that will listen. They do not find it among some Christians, because these Christians are talking where they

should be listening. But they who can no longer listen to others will soon be no longer listening to God either; . . . One who cannot listen long and patiently will presently be talking beside the point and be never really speaking to others, albeit he be not conscious of it. Anyone who thinks that his time is too valuable to spend keeping quiet will eventually have no time for God or others, but only for himself and his own follies. There is a kind of listening with half an ear that presumes already to know what the other has to say. It is impatient, inattentive litening (*Life Together*, pp. 87–88).

Meditation

Jesus had a conversation with a Samaritan woman at Jacob's well. Here is the last part of that conversation:

> *The woman said to him, I know that Messiah is coming (who is called Christ). When he comes, he will proclaim all things to us. Jesus said to her, I am he, the one who is speaking to you. Just then his disciples came. They were astonished that he was speaking with a woman, but no one said, What do you want? or Why are you speaking with her?* (John 4:25–26).

- ☞ With whom do you have your best conversations? Why? What happens between you and this person that makes the interaction special?

- ☞ Reflect on your conversations with others. Do you feel you are a good listener? What makes a good listener?

- ☞ What can you do to nurture another person through conversation?

- ☞ Do you think of prayer as conversation between yourself and God? If so, sit quietly for a few minutes and notice how that prayerful conversation with God unfolds right now. Are you speaking or listening?

Worship

Worshippers . . . keep the Sabbath holy
in a joyful celebration of Christ's resurrection.

Dorothy C. Bass

I FEEL THE MOST TOTALLY ENGAGED IN WORSHIP through music, especially choral music and congregational singing during worship. Years ago at Luther College, when I sang bass in the chapel choir, I learned to appreciate sacred choral music, including Gregorian chant. I love the great traditional hymns of the Church that are part of my heritage. During the worship service, when I am singing a hymn accompanied by a great pipe organ, I sometimes unexpectedly choke up as a feeling of overwhelming joy and meaning comes to me.

I often feel close to God in the solitude of a mountain, but as Marjorie Thompson says, "It is impossible to be Christian in solitary splendor." I need corporate worship with others. I can worship in a variety of church settings, and I have—but for me, the most meaningful worship experience usually includes a full liturgy, great hymns accompanied by a pipe organ, a good sermon and Eucharist.

My home community, Holden Lutheran Church, is a place where worship often reminds me of my groundedness. I am aware as I kneel at the altar rail to receive the Lord's Supper that I am only a few feet removed from where I was baptized many years ago. I cross myself as a physical reminder of being sealed by baptism for life everlasting into the union of the Father, Son and Holy Spirit. Communion reminds me and confirms for me that we are a part of the community, not solitary and private Christians.

There are a wide range of worship formats and options. While my preference is the liturgical setting of the Lutherans or the Anglicans, where the common lectionary texts are read and preached, I have also worshiped in and appreciate many non-liturgical and informal settings.

Seattle, *September 22, 2001*

I went to a large Presbyterian Church the week after the tragic events of September 11, 2001. The church was full, and the preaching was powerful, as was the music. The worship was inspirational, and I trust that for all those present it was a moving worship experience, as it was for me. Even though I was inspired, I also felt anonymous and small. It can be hard to feel a part of the community in a large church, at least as a visitor. Yet, in contrast, when I asked my son Daniel about his attendance at worship, he said that he prefers anonymity rather than too much "welcoming of the visitor" or a passing of the peace that turns out to be a brief social mixer in the middle of worship. Daniel is not a regular congregant in a church, so I listen to and respect his opinion.

Tatranska Lomnica, Slovakia, *Sunday, October 14, 2007*

I am here to run a workshop for about 20 Heifer International country staff members, most of whom are trainers from all around Eastern and Central Europe. Though we are from ten different countries and speak several languages, we bond quickly and form a strong group because of our dedication to a common mission and our similar values of service. I have been retired from Heifer for several years but was recently asked to write a book for field staff on values-based development. This has been published and distributed to program staff all over the world. I am here now to review this method with these regional trainers who will take it back to their teammates. I am having lots of fun in the process.

Years ago when I first joined the Heifer staff at headquarters, the organization had a more explicit Christian identity then it does today. We frequently started our staff meetings and retreats with prayer and devotions. In recent years, Heifer has grown significantly and in the process has moved toward a more secular identity, though maintaining a broad-based understanding of spirituality. They continue to do impressive work toward achieving the mission of ending world hunger.

As a trainer with Heifer, I almost always incorporated devotionals into the workshop schedule, being sensitive to the faith traditions of the participants. As this workshop commenced, I announced that I would be leading a short devotional—a kind of worship experience—on Sunday morning. I indicated that any who wished to come voluntarily would be most welcome. A staff member from Azerbaijan was curious. He said he had never heard of a devotional and doesn't know what it is but thought it would be interesting to attend as an observer. I invited him to come.

On Sunday morning a small group gathered—eight of us in total—Judy, Greta, Anahit, Knarine, Grazina, Sergey, Yaroslava and me. We sat in a circle and used the lectio divina approach to scripture reading and prayer, slowly reading a scripture text followed by silence—repeating this several times until each had read the text in their own language. Several participants had brought their Bibles, and we read the great commandment of Jesus from Matthew 22: 36–40. Each read aloud in their own language: Armenian, Lithuanian, Russian, Ukrainian and English. While we listened to words we didn't understand, we knew the message by heart, and in this way we prayed in other tongues. Each one then shared a bit of application of this text from their particular context. Yaroslava from Ukraine was perhaps the most devout of the group, though limited in her ability to express thoughts and feelings in English. Greta, the American who speaks Russian, interpreted for her as she told us something of her story. She said her mother was exiled to a prison camp in Siberia for 16 years. Yaroslava was born there. Her mother was her spiritual hero and inspiration. Grazina, from Lithuania, was an attractive middle-aged woman with a somewhat melancholy demeanor and a peaceful presence. She was the only one besides Judy and me who came from a Lutheran tradition. The Armenians were from the Armenian Orthodox Church, one of the oldest churches in the world. From previous experience in Armenia, I knew there has been very little liturgical renewal in that church, but Anahit and Knarine are devout and were lively in sharing their faith.

These and all of the other workshop participants lived their formative years in communist countries in which religion and worship were repressed. It is for this reason that many of them may not have been exposed to religious education or

Christian worship. Each of those gathered for worship talked of their difficulty as well as their joy in following Jesus' great commandment. In those few moments together I felt we were intensely united in worship as part of the Body of Christ. We concluded our time together praying the Lord's Prayer, each in our own language.

—◆—

When in Latin America I frequently go into a Catholic church when I have free time or when I feel a special need for prayer, quietness and reverence. Sometimes I attend Mass. But whether or not corporate worship is underway, I find that the Catholic Church offers a sense of reverence and quietude, more so than do the Evangelical and Pentecostal houses of worship. In Catholic churches people usually sit or kneel in prayer, sometimes praying a personal litany or reciting the rosary. Congregants prepare themselves for the celebration of the Eucharist. I learned long ago to value a time of quiet before the worship service begins and am often irritated at chatting and conversation as people loudly enter a church prior to worship.

In some of the more ornate and well-known churches of Latin America and Europe, tourists wander around, delighting in the beautiful architecture and art. They do not seem to be there for worship, though how can I judge what is in their hearts. Maybe it is a worshipful experience they seek. I've done the same thing—wander in for a look as a tourist.

I may be getting more and more out of sync with the cultural patterns of our day as so many churches take up "contemporary" worship, often accompanied by incessant noise and activity before, during and at the conclusion of the service. In Pentecostal churches in Latin America, I can appreciate the enthusiasm and passion of the worshipers, but it definitely is not my style.

San Salvador, February, 2006

Today I found myself in San Salvador on a Sunday morning with a desire to find a community and attend worship. It was February 10—the Transfiguration of our Lord. With my friends Norma and Greg I walked to a nearby Pentecostal

48

family service and sauntered in. The instant the service began we were inundated with sound—an elevated volume for prayers, preaching, and songs, amplified instrumental music, clapping and singing. It was very loud! The prayers with arms swinging high above heads were emotional pleas and petitions to the Lord. There was also much giving of thanks to the Lord (*Gracias a Dios!*). I left after an hour—hoping to diminish the possibility of hearing damage.

In contrast, I then went to a modern Catholic Church in the same neighborhood, a Mass well-attended by many young families. The priest spoke about salt and light of the earth, that which gives flavor and sight to us for this life. Worship here was more familiar and calming to my soul and senses. No one introduced themselves, and I was only momentarily a part of that community. Yet it was an edifying and enriching worship for me this Sunday morning.

Once when I was in Tegucigalpa I went to a Mass with Tim and Gloria at the *Iglesia de los Dolorosas*. In the middle of the sermon, a man sitting alone a few pews in front of us suffered an epileptic seizure. By the manner of his dress he was obviously a poor man. He was immediately attended by several of the worshippers seated around him, who soothed and massaged him until his body relaxed and he was released from his seizure. Observing this drama left me with a sense of empathy followed by personal prayer for this poor man. I actually felt a tension rising in my body and then a calming as he revived. It was a joy to have worshiped and communed here though I knew none of the congregants personally with the exception of Tim and Gloria. I nonetheless experienced a response of attentiveness that came with being a part of the Holy Catholic Church—the Church Universal.

Tirana, Albania, October, 1997

On Sunday morning in Tirana, Albania: I went looking for the Orthodox Church. I had not found this church the previous week and had ended up in the Roman Catholic Church, which was fine. This morning I did find the Orthodox cathedral and went in. As in most Orthodox churches I have visited in Eastern Europe, there is little seating available. So I stood in the back behind the pews for almost an hour, and I experienced what was one of the most beautiful liturgies I have ever heard, especially considering the fact that I didn't understand a word of it. All the senses are involved in this worship. There was wonderful chanting and choir music by a dozen priests adorned in colorful and intricately woven stoles, capes and gowns. The one who appeared to be the bishop was the most elaborately attired with a high hat, ornately decorated, and wearing numerous crosses around his neck. He came into the assembly with acolytes casting incense in every direction. The chanting seemed to be harmonic and mono-tonal at the same time. There were filigree-carved wooden partitions between the sanctuary where the congregation stood and the altar. This partition is called an *iconostasis*.

As time passed I was aware that the crowd around me was growing as the church slowly filled with worshipers, many times genuflecting and staying on their knees on that concrete floor for what seemed an excruciatingly long time. At one point the choir and congregation—most of them—sang continuously for about ten minutes without the aid of hymnals. They knew the whole liturgy from memory. It was a feast for the senses, indeed, and I felt the presence of Christ. Though I did not understand a word of their language, I knew the Word was among us and within me. Indeed, worship is an experience that transcends the limits of language.

Reflection

Marjorie Thompson writes this about worship:

> For many people, private worship is more attractive than public worship. Envisioning faith as a private affair reflects the individualism of our culture. Many ask why corporate worship should be so important when they can meditate on God in nature with far less distraction.

> The reasons for gathering are many and important. Whether we are alone or with others, we need to experience our Christian life as rooted in the larger community of faith. Even our most personal disciplines need to be supported, broadened, clarified and sometimes corrected in the light of corporate theology and practice. Otherwise we are susceptible to privatized visions of spiritual truths. Moreover, we need the prayers of

others as they need our prayers. The way God provides for our deepest hopes is through the hands and hearts of others (*Soul Feast: An Invitation to the Christian Spiritual Life*, pp. 55, 56).

Meditation

O come, let us worship and bow down, let us kneel before the Lord, our Maker! For he is our God, and we are the people of his pasture, and the sheep of his hand.

Psalm 95: 6,7

☞ How important is regular corporate worship to you? In what ways does it nourish you?

☞ If you are not active in a Christian community, what prevents you from attending?

☞ Assuming that you attend worship that offers the sacrament of Holy Communion, what is it in that sacrament that is most meaningful to you?

☞ In many denominations participation in worship has decreased in recent years. Why do you think this is so? Are you hopeful about the future of the Church? Why?

Silence

Silence is the discipline by which the inner fire of God
is tended and kept alive.

Henry Nouwen

I ONCE WAS ASKED TO SPEAK to a church group about daily encounters with God. I suggested to the group that they visualize a time and place when they had felt particularly close to God. After that visualization I asked how many of them had during this exercise gone in their mind's eyes to a worship service in a church and how many went to other places, such as a place of silence in nature. A good number of hands went up indicating they had gone to a quiet spot in nature. I think back to such times in my own experience . . .

En route to Nepal, September, 1998

I had been sitting on an airplane for 15 hours on my way to Nepal. This question came to me: When was I first aware of the presence of God in my life? I honestly cannot remember a specific time—it must have grown on me unaware. But one event that comes to my consciousness is the 1955 Lutheran youth convention I attended in San Francisco. I was entering my senior year in high school that fall. There were 8,000 young people at that convention! I remember the night we were asked to keep silence from the time we left the evening session until the following morning. The verse we were left with was *Be still, and know that I am God* from Psalm 46. We filed out of the large arena mostly keeping our mouths shut and our eyes averted from others. Not exactly silence, however, as the sound of thousands of shuffling feet on the concrete stairs was pronounced. I was determined to follow the instructions even though some of my housemates could not keep quiet that night.

Why do I remember such an obscure event? I suppose because it was so startling and out of the ordinary, and I wanted to be obedient and follow Christ at that particular time, or at least to obey the instructions of the pastors in charge. Certainly there was a degree of piety in my upbringing—and I had always been taught to bow your head, close your eyes and pray—but never in my experience until that moment had I been encouraged to pray in silence for more than a moment at a time. I had no idea that there was a 2,000-year history of such a practice.

The first time I can remember observing silence intentionally as a spiritual practice was at a retreat near Little Rock in 1981. Our friends Jim and Ervin Bullock had attended a silent retreat at the Church of the Savior in Washington D.C. They came back and recommended that our small support group try our own silent retreat. I had not heard of such a thing and could barely imagine what value there would be in spending a whole weekend together in silence. I had always been keen on discussing and sharing ideas and feelings or singing and praying aloud with others. For me, prayer had always been mental—spoken or read prayers with words usually verbalized by someone else. I went into the weekend with great curiosity and kept track of my thoughts and feelings in my journal.

Friday night, Fall of 1981

During the first 15 minutes after the silent part of the retreat commenced, I noticed certain sounds in my environment. What happened first surprised me a bit. As soon as Ervin finished a scripture reading, almost everyone got up and started moving about, as if they knew where they were going. I just sat still and stayed where I was. What I heard in the silence were echoes: David's laughter, Lon's wisecracks, then raucous laughter of the whole group . . . fun along with some anxious questions. What do we do with the silence? What are the rules? What is supposed to happen? What's the purpose?

I was fortunate to have had a few moments of conversation with Jim earlier in the evening. His comments and description of the Church of the Savior experience made sense to me. He talked about the inward journey as a process. It is not just about running after every need or interesting idea that comes to mind. Rather the focus should first be on what God is calling me to be and do. The Church of the

Savior encourages members to look at ministry as calling, lifting up a concern or ministry that one is drawn to and that may also attract a few other sojourners. So this first silence experience focused on discernment of ministry and God's will. Many thoughts and reflections went through my mind that weekend. The sounds of the day kept intruding, and the sounds of my inner mind kept up a constant buzz of analysis. I had not yet heard about meditation and contemplation in the Christian tradition.

⟨⟩

Since then, I have read numerous books and been in retreats and heard talks on meditation and contemplative prayer that highlight the importance of silence in the spiritual life. There are various terms in use: centering prayer, meditation, lectio divina and contemplation. I have come to understand both meditation and contemplation as forms of prayer in a long tradition of centering in silence in the presence of God's Spirit. Contemplation has a long and ancient history in the Christian tradition.

Meditation is a term used both in the Christian and Eastern traditions. On the surface the various practices of meditation seem to have similarities—whether from the East or the West. But a prolific writer on the subject of prayer, Joyce Huggett, clarifies how meditation and contemplation are understood in the Christian tradition. She says the word—meditate—used in the Psalms, means to mutter or to murmur persistently:

> Christian mediation must not be confused with yoga, Eastern meditation or transcendental meditation. For, unlike these disciplines, Christian meditation has nothing to do with emptying our minds. Christian meditation engages every part of us—our mind, our emotions, our imaginations, our creativity and, supremely, our will. The word, meditation, (as used in various Psalms) means "to muse," "to ponder" and "to consider." In other words, Christian meditation involves not emptiness, but fullness.
> It means being attentive to God.

By contrast, she writes:

> Contemplation goes further and deeper than meditation. While the

54

person meditating mutters and muses on God's word, the contemplative pays silent attention to Jesus, the living Word—the one who is central to their prayer. Indeed, contemplation goes one step further. Contemplation goes beyond words and symbols and concepts to the reality the words and concepts describe (Huggett, quoted on pages 13 and 14 of Richard Foster's book *Spiritual Classics*).

A form of contemplative prayer that has been popularized in recent decades is called centering prayer. In centering prayer the participant chooses a word that settles into one's heart, such as peace, Jesus, love, etc. Once I even heard a nun say that her word was "nothing" since that is what she wanted going through her mind during silent contemplative prayer . . . "nothing . . . nothing more than loving God." Most writers recommend picking a prayer word and sticking with it. The word recommended by the British Benedictine, John Main, was "Mar-a-na-tha." The translation of the word *maranatha*, is "Come O Lord," and I often use this as my sacred word, but it is not the only word that moves me toward contemplation.

In looking back at my journal entries over the years, I find many references to times of quiet and wonder, especially during travels to numerous beautiful locations in the world for Heifer International during the 1990s. On these trips, I usually conducted training workshops for local staff, and I often had the leisure of taking time in the mornings for silence before sessions started. Sometimes there were additional opportunities to take breaks in serene and peaceful settings.

South Africa, January, 1998

I am privileged to find myself in a game park in South Africa—taking a few days break after a long and strenuous trip through Zimbabwe, Mozambique and South Africa. We had the unexpected delight of ending up in a park where there were practically no other tourists and with exceptional accommodations compared to our usual fare on these travels. We had a bush lodge all to ourselves—incredible! We stayed in cabins in a verdant forest surrounded by luxuriant foliage. This was a place of peace and harmony with the natural world: the sounds, sights and feel of creation the way it is intended to be. To sit on the veranda in the evening or early morning was the essence of peacefulness. The singing birds, the running water in the nearby ravine and many sounds of animals in the forest were our constant background, our sounds of silence.

We had our own cook and a game warden who led us on several treks through the bush, walking as silently as possible, following our guide's hand signals. When we came upon a herd of White Rhinos, I was transfixed, and I kept as still as I could ever imagine myself being, while at the same time experiencing an adrenalin rush.

How restful it was to sleep in such a place, waking up during the night to the gentle sound of rain on the roof and the songs and chirping of birds in the trees in the early morning. At supper we heard the moaning cry of a lion in the distance and the laugh of a hyena. The nyalas, brown, medium-sized hoofed antelope with thin white stripes, were grazing near the cabin this morning. I watched them wake up, slowly move off and start to graze. We looked at each other with wide smiles as if to say, "It doesn't get any better than this." I wish I could write as well as the psalmists . . . "The heavens proclaim the glory of God!" and "Be still, and know that I am God!" It was relatively easy for me to sit in silence for a long time in the early morning or evening in such a setting. It was a kind of reverence before the glory of nature that calls us to silence ourselves in wonder.

———◆◆———

We should not be too adamant about finding a precise definition of meditation and contemplation. Different writers define these terms in different ways. Was this experience in the game park meditation or contemplation? Does it really matter what it is called? I do know it was a time of peace and being in relationship with the Creator.

On February 15, 1998, I made a note about the book I was reading. William Menninger's book, *The Loving Search for God*, is the best I have read on contemplative prayer. It is based on a fourteenth century classic by an unknown author, entitled *The Cloud of Unknowing*. "Now I must set aside twenty minutes a day," I wrote. "I am much attracted to contemplative prayer, especially growing in a loving relationship with God, not just knowing more *about* God."

Yet no matter how drawn I have been to silence and contemplative prayer over these years, I have never adopted centering prayer as a consistent daily spiritual

56

practice. There may have been only a few dozen times when I have intentionally sat in such a state of complete and uninterrupted silence for 30 minutes, though there have been many times when I have enjoyed the peace and quiet of the forest or mountain, sitting in wordless appreciation or, at times, sitting completely silent in a small group.

Here is the method of centering prayer I have learned and practiced in several settings:

> Choose a place where you are not liable to be interrupted for some minutes. Sit in a chair or on a pillow on the floor with your back straight. In the sitting position keep your feet flat on the floor. Close your eyes with your head held comfortably and center yourself with hands loosely folded in your lap.
>
> Breathe deeply and slowly, filling your lungs by expanding your abdomen. As you begin, you may want to say a brief prayer asking for the presence of the Spirit during this time. Choose your prayer word and stick with that word, repeating it as you breathe in and out. If this contemplative session is in a group, the leader indicates the starting time and may read a short verse of Scripture or say a prayer.
>
> Those who teach the centering prayer method recommend keeping silence for twenty minutes. One should not feel guilty if the period is shorter, but try for at least eight or ten minutes. It is certain that you will experience distractions. When distractions come, either external sounds or internal thoughts, memories and other mental messages, simply continue to repeat your prayer word. Do not whisper or mouth your word; simply let it repeat itself in you with each deep breath. Do not fret or struggle to keep thoughts at bay, simply let them pass gently through you and disappear. An image that is sometimes used is that of a leaf falling off a tree and gently flowing past and floating to the ground as you let it go. At some point you may realize you are not repeating your prayer word, but simply resting in silence in the loving arms of God.

If it does happen that you fall asleep, when you awaken, simply go back to your word and continue in silent repose, loving God without words. If you are in a group, the leader will indicate when the time is up by softly voicing a prayer. Take a minute or two to transition back to the present, open your eyes and enjoy the here and now.

Reflection

By the Pond

As I sit by the pond in silence,

a solitary bird chirps and then flies away.

Just as there is seldom complete darkness

there is seldom complete silence.

I have known moments of silence, more here than for awhile.

I am still and content to be here for the moment, but . . .

Now a million raindrops quietly fall on the surface of the water.

The birds pause for a moment—deep silence.

It's time to go inside.

Silence always comes and goes—it never stays.

Pecos Benedictine Monastery, September, 2009

Meditation

*Now during those days he went out to the mountain to pray;
and he spent the night in prayer to God.*

Luke 6:12

☞ Find a comfortable position, close your eyes and focus on a time
when you were aware of the presence of God? Open all your senses
to that moment—your feelings, the sounds, aromas, temperature,
lighting, surroundings.

☞ By nature, are you a person who is comfortable with silence? If so,
what do you like about silence? If not, what could you do to allow
yourself to experiment with moments of silence?

☞ Try the Centering Prayer method described above by releasing
thoughts from your mind and allowing yourself to sit in silence for
up to ten minutes. Words are not necessary—just be silent in the
presence of God.

☞ Finally, take a moment to write something in your journal about
your time of silence. Do you feel a desire to structure a routine of
silence at some time each day or week?

Pray—Without Ceasing?

After saying farewell to them,
he went up on the mountain to pray.

John 6:46

Little Rock, Arkansas, *January, 1998*

My friend Darrell gave me this Celtic prayer which draws me back to my center
and reminds me to put first things first as I plan for the year.

> Circle me, O God—Keep hope within, keep despair without
>
> Circle me, O God—Keep peace within, keep turmoil without
>
> Circle me, O God—Keep calm within, keep storms without
>
> Circle me, O God—Keep strength within, keep weakness out

One of my constant prayers is for patience and discernment, and I should add
to that inner peace. I need this now as I have planned a heavy travel schedule to
countries that were such an important part of my past. I pray for stamina to do
this much traveling and to be separated again for so much of the year from Judy.
What a wonderful life partner I have—I am thankful.

St. Paul advises us, *Rejoice always, pray without ceasing* (1 Thessalonians 5:16, 17).

To be honest, I would say that I am not doing that. It seems impractical and
unrealistic. But is it possible that we are in prayer and not even aware of it?
Besides this question, there are many others about prayer that come to mind.
The most common is "Does God answer prayer?"

Recently I visited in the home of a Mennonite family who live on a farm in Saskatchewan, Canada—a young couple and their two small sons. The grandparents lived in the main house on the same property. The grandfather had been suffering for months from a very painful illness, and the family held him in prayer every day. But there had been little improvement in his condition. At breakfast one morning, we enjoyed a time of conversation and sharing about our lives, and the subject turned to prayer. We talked about this question of God's answering prayer, and they said they had recently discussed this with the boys and posed the question of whether we listen to God or just continuously make our petitions and intercessions—the communication going all in one direction.

Little Kevin spoke up and said, "Yes, I listened and heard God's answer." The parents were curious to know what Kevin had heard. He said, "God said, 'Don't worry, your grandpa is going to be alright. I'm doing the best I can.'"

Let the application be made by parents, theologians and all who wonder about this question.

⇒•⇐

Henri Nouwen wrote about noticing and assessing the results of prayer:

> What is most close, most intimate, most present, often cannot be experienced directly, but only with a certain distance. . . . I wonder if in this sense I am not participating in what the apostles experienced. When Jesus was with them, they could not fully realize or understand what was happening. Only after he had left did they sense, feel and understand how close he really had been to them (*The Genesee Dairy: Report from a Trappist Monastery*, p. 141).

Nouwen makes the point that many have wondered about, that it often seems that nothing happens when we pray. But when we stay with it and look back over a period of time, we realize that something has happened. We may not recognize God's actions in our lives when we are too close to the action. Only by looking back in retrospect and remembering the content of our recent prayers do we become aware of the good that came out of a particular situation. One method of noticing is to journal. Journaling helps bring our daily struggles and experiences to consciousness and helps remind us of God's presence and answers to prayer.

Benedictine School and Seminary, near Quetzaltenango, Guatemala, August 14, 2002

When I arrived, I noticed the logo of the Benedictine monks on the wall of the seminary is *"A todos los huéspedes que se presentan, se les recibirá como a Cristo."* (To all guests who present themselves, receive them as if they are Christ).

I am in a perfect setting for a retreat. I went to bed early and slept well, falling to sleep with the sound of thunder and rain. It was very quiet until 5:45 a.m. when the ringing of bells called the students and monks to morning prayers. I decided to get up and join them at six o'clock. I didn't find the right book to follow the readings and prayers, yet I appreciated being there. Listening to the readings and prayers was sufficient for the moment. This is part of their daily practice, part of the rule of Saint Benedict.

Then I went to the library of the monastery and happened to pick a book off the shelf about *flow*—a term used in psychology and in Buddhism. The hallmark of flow is a feeling of spontaneous joy while performing a task. Other terms used are *in the moment, present, in the zone, in the groove or keeping your head in the game.* Flow seems to have to do with being right with your inner and outer world at the same time. It is having a sense that things happen for a reason. I don't remember much more about it.

Shortly after this I experienced a curious coincidence—in fact two of them.

One: After breakfast I went on a walk to take in the fresh, crisp air of the Guatemalan highlands and to enjoy a view of the volcanoes and surrounding mountains. Walking in a quiet place helps me to center myself for the day. It is good to take a break before going into the intensity of the workshop. I walked to the end of the driveway and arrived at that spot exactly at the same time as old friends Joe and Salena Keeseker came walking down the road. I had not seen them for several years, and though I knew they were now Presbyterian missionaries in Guatemala, I had no idea where they were living. Was this pure coincidence? We were surprised by joy, to use a phrase from C.S. Lewis. We greeted each other with much *alegría* (joy) and chatted animatedly for as long as we could before we each headed into our day's activities. As I looked back on it later, it seemed to be a moment of God-given grace.

Two: As I was preparing for the day I wanted to find the Isaiah text related to the vision of a New Jerusalem. I needed some inspiration from the Word. I generally don't know verse and chapter in the Bible by memory so I looked through the book of Isaiah. But I could not locate what I was looking for and gave up on the idea. I had wanted to use that text to lead a visioning session with the Presbyterian Church organization I am working with this week. When we assembled and sat down to begin the session, I had my Bible on my lap, and it fell open to Isaiah 65. My eyes went right to verse 17 where the vision text begins. Was it a coincidence, or dare I think of it as the prompting of the Spirit?

———◆———

This all may sound like new age spirituality—the business about flow and coincidences. But as I reviewed the day, I looked back on these experiences as somehow Spirit led. I did not silently verbalize prayers all day long, nor was I in voiced adoration, song or worship after the time of morning prayers. The workshop went well, and I felt it was a day of gentle receptiveness and a kind of being in the flow and in the presence of God. Perhaps this was an example of simultaneity that Quaker writer Thomas Kelly wrote about when he stated:

> There is a way of ordering our mental life on more than one level at once. On one level we may be thinking, discussing, seeing, calculating, and meeting all the demands of external affairs. But deep within, behind the scenes, at a more profound level, we may also be in prayer and adoration, song and worship and a gentle receptiveness to divine breathings.

> . . . at first the practice of inward prayer is a process of alternation of attention. We are either in the outer world of activity and consciousness or given to the Inner Light. We are not aware that we can be in both at the same time. The first signs of simultaneity are when, as we slow down from activity and thought, it dawns on us that "we have not completely

forgotten God"—we seem to have a vague sense that the Spirit is present (*A Testament of Devotion*, p. 13).

Speaking of his own practice of intercessory prayer, William Temple, once an archbishop of Canterbury, said, "When I pray, coincidences happen, and when I do not pray, they don't."

When my friend Janis Hansen read this chapter she remarked, "Spirituality is when the inner and the outer in one's life mesh."

Sometimes I am preoccupied and thinking deeply about something or someone—perhaps having an internal dialogue with someone. This may be a time of intense emotions, deep questioning, or wondering "Why?" It may be a nagging worry for a loved one who is going through a crisis. I am not explicitly praying or even aware of the Other one until at some future moment I look back on that time and become conscious of it as prayer.

The monastery, *continued*

It was a good day! It was a chance to do a retreat and at the same time an opportunity to serve and use my experience in strategic planning and visioning with an organization that greatly needs help. I am concerned and even a bit irritated with Jorge, the leader, for his pessimistic attitude, and I have been looking for a positive approach that will turn him around, making him able to provide good leadership. I have heard from him and others about internal conflicts and struggles in the church, so there is need for renewal and repentance! I pray for wisdom, understanding and patience. With God's help I will do as much as I can with the time and people available. Throughout the day, participation was good, and we achieved better than expected results, I think.

In the evening I joined the students and brothers again for vespers. The discipline and reverence of classic prayers is a blessing. I felt myself to be in the presence and grace of God with these brothers. There is something relaxing about being led in prayer this way.

The Diaconia staff's work of writing plans and objectives went on into the night while I retreated to my room. During the night my sleep was interrupted by dreams and wakefulness, much pondering and thought. A long period in silent prayer in the chapel in the morning was calming. There are some places and times where praying happens constantly, and it is good and useful to be in a place when this happens naturally.

Reflection

Several years ago I attended a prayer workshop led by Jane Vennard, who teaches prayer and spiritual practices. She talked about how hard it is for church members to talk about prayer with each other. She feels that many have not learned how to pray. In her book she says she believes that:

> . . . anything we do that honors, strengthens or deepens our relationship to God can become a form of prayer. Does this mean that anything we do can become a prayer? Yes, but everything is not automatically a prayer. To fashion our actions into prayers, we need to examine our intentions for the activity and God's intention for us . . . When we broaden our concept of prayer, we are able to be attentive to God during much of our daily activities. I believe that making all we do a form of prayer is what the apostle Paul meant when he told his disciples to pray without ceasing (*A Praying Congregation*, pp. 45, 46).

Meditation

Rejoice always. Pray without ceasing; give thanks in all circumstances; for this is the will of God in Christ Jesus for you.

I Thessalonians 5:16–18

☞ What is your personal reaction to and experience with Thomas Kelly's notion of simultaneity, quoted in this chapter?

☞ Is there a characteristic pattern to your prayers, e.g., prayers of petition, intercession for others, praise and thankfulness, or confession?

☞ When you take the long view of prayer and review your life, you may see that prayers have been answered, but you were not aware of it in the immediacy of the moment. Reflect on an instance in retrospect, when you felt your prayers were answered, even though you may not have realized it at the time.

Spontaneous Contemplation

*The apostles gathered around Jesus, and told him all that they had done
and taught. He said to them, "Come away to a deserted place all by
your selves, and rest awhile."*

Mark 6:30, 31

The Bay Islands, Honduras, *February, 1997*

After a week of training with the Heifer team, Judy joined me for a trip to the Bay
Islands to celebrate her fifty-fifth birthday. We were here once about 20 years ago,
but, oh, how this place has changed!

We sat on a beach in West Bay watching the sunset. Contemplation is like a
sunset . . . we realize how beautiful it is at the moment it happens, and at the very
same time, we know it will only stay with us for a few brief moments. It passes
but leaves an inner calm and glow.

We are staying at the *Bannanarama cabanas,* owned and run by a young German
couple, and we are enjoying a truly relaxing and low stress time together. There
is nothing to decide here except what pleasures of this natural paradise we want
to experience next. We talk, pray, dialogue, read and have times of quietness and
silence together, besides walking on the beach, swimming, making love, running,
diving, eating and even fasting.

Jurgen offered to teach me something about scuba diving and took me out into
the coral reef not far out from the beach. I had done lots of snorkeling in the
various tropical locations where we have lived and traveled, but never scuba diving.

Recently I have read much about meditation and contemplation and have made
some attempts to practice it. Scuba diving and snorkeling are marvelous object

67

lessons. One of the descriptions of contemplation is to simply be empty of thoughts and let oneself rest in the arms of God in quietude, realizing that this may occur only for fleeting moments and that this is not explainable in words. Nevertheless, I will try to describe it. . . .

Out in the water I simply relaxed and floated around, gazing at the beauty of creation: multi-colored fish swimming by in schools, coral, tiny sea insects, eels, seaweed, rock formations—incredible, almost incomparable beauty. The sunlight streamed through from above; the color, shapes, and motion all came together at the same time and brought about a sense of sheer contentment. I was simply there—not to touch or hold—but to be in the presence of this wonder of nature. I suppose I was somehow aware of the creator and of creation at the same time as I gazed at the beauty of these unusual formations. I was aware of being alone with God in that place of splendor but unaware at that time of anything else but the magnificence surrounding me. No words needed, no spoken prayers, no thinking . . . only an occasional utterance of "awesome!" and laughter into my mask. Somehow I was fixed on a mysterious *other* while still aware of myself as a part of that design.

—————◆—————

In his study of the lives of John of the Cross and Theresa de Avila, Gerald May gives a clear description of the classical Christian use of the two terms meditation and contemplation. These two saints are often quoted mystics from sixteenth-century Spain. John of the Cross is famous for giving us the term *the dark night of the soul*, which May says is often misunderstood in modern times:

> Put simply, meditation is what we seem to be able to do and accomplish on our own, while contemplation is what seems to come as sheer gift. To use John's words, meditation includes all the "acts and exercises" of prayer and spiritual practice—the things one does intentionally. In contrast, contemplation cannot be practiced. . . . for contemplation is entirely God's gift of grace. It cannot be achieved or acquired. It happens when it happens. . . . In a larger sense, meditation applies to all intentional prayer. . . . It can take any number of forms: from delving into Scripture

to repeating a holy word, from journaling to liturgical dancing, from inward visualizations to simply going through the day with mindfulness (*The Dark Night of the Soul,* pp. 107, 108).

This description by Gerald May comes close to a characterization of my experience in the water, perhaps a bit akin to how Carl Jung used the sense of being under the water as analogous to the unconscious, and we might say, to the soul.

Southern Poland, *June 4, 1998*

I am here to help the Heifer staff from Central and Eastern Europe learn how to conduct a country program review and evaluation. After our session yesterday, we took a magnificent ride by horse-drawn carriage for two hours in the forest. There was much laughter, conversation, and appreciation of the beauty of nature all about us on our little outing, as we breathed in grand vistas of mountains, meadows and trees. As Thomas Mann put it, "the voice of nature mingles with that of man and over all lies the bright-eyed freshness of the new day!"

The text from the daily lectionary this morning was Psalm 8. This is one of my favorites, and it contains appropriate sentiments for today: *When I look at your heavens, the work of your fingers, the moon and the stars that you have established: What are human beings that you are mindful of them, mortals (sons and daughters of humankind) that you care for them?* After the hilarity of the evening I have a chance to sit in silence. As I look into the starlit skies tonight I feel close to all that is around me . . . the company of good friends, full of good food and drink, the splendor of creation all about. Yes, O Lord, how majestic is your name in all the earth!

Lake Atitlan, Guatemala, *April 20, 2001*

I arise at 5:30 am and sit on the bench in front of my little *cabaña*. I brought my Bible to read but decide to just sit here and take in the silence as the new day unfolds. The picture before my eyes is perfect. It is hard to imagine a place more peaceful and serene where I could contemplate more fully. I write these words, even though I realize my grasp is only a tiny glimpse of the scene and its originator—the Divine One.

Two large volcanoes, Atitlan and Toliman, are right there—I feel as if I could almost reach out and touch them. The lake in front of me is like a shimmering mirror; I hear the birds singing but no sounds from the lake below where a canoe carrying a single person glides silently across the surface. I realize I cannot fully appreciate this moment—my words are not adequate to describe my contemplation. Even as I am aware of the beauty of and preciousness of the moment, it is changing and moving on into the new day. I utter a prayer of praise and thanksgiving—Oh Lord Creator, how great is your majesty and mystery. I ask the Spirit to imprint this moment and vision on my brain to help me to know and remind me at some later time of the holiness and grandeur of creation. I look up Psalm 121 and read it, slowly. This is a time of worship, though a very solitary one.

———

Jane Goodall, the world famous scientist, environmentalist, and defender of animals, wrote about her contemplative experience in Notre Dame Cathedral. Her life and career has had tremendous positive influence on millions of people. She wrote these words in her memoir:

> Many years ago, in the spring of 1974, I visited the cathedral of Notre Dame in Paris. There were not many people around, and it was quiet and still inside. I gazed in silent awe at the great Rose Window, glowing in the morning sun. All at once the cathedral was filled with a huge volume of sound: an organ playing magnificently for a wedding taking place in a distant corner: Bach's Toccata and Fugue in D Minor. I had always loved the opening theme; but in the cathedral, filling the entire vastness, it seemed to enter and possess my whole self. It was as though the music itself was alive. That moment, a suddenly captured moment of eternity, was perhaps the closest I have ever come to experiencing ecstasy, the ecstasy of the mystic. How could I believe it was the chance gyrations of bits of primeval dust that had led up to that moment in time—the cathedral soaring to the sky; the collective inspiration and faith of those who caused it to be built; the advent of Bach himself, his brain that translated truth into music; and the mind that could, as mine did then, comprehend the whole inexorable progression of evolution? Since I cannot believe that this was the result of chance, I have to admit to anti-

chance. And so I must believe in the guiding power in the universe—in other words, I must believe in God (*Reason for Hope: A Spiritual Journey,* p. 288).

If there is anyone who has been on an endless journey in the pursuit of showing truth and hope to a world mired in a seemingly hopeless abyss of conflict, environmental degradation, and greed, it is Jane Goodall. She has gone through periods of doubt, suffered deep pain at the death of loved ones, and has been close to victims of cruelty, both animals and humans. Yet, she says "most of the time I am optimistic about the future," and she gives of herself from a deep well.

I choose to call these examples (mine and one from Jane Goodall) spontaneous contemplation. These experiences of mystic union with God come at unexpected times and places. Is it arrogant and presumptuous to think that we might be so close to God as to feel with all our being that God is within us and all around us at a given moment in time? Reflecting on her experience at Notre Dame twenty years later, Jane Goodall writes about what happened that day in the cathedral, "It came at a time when so much was changing in my life. . . . When I was, without knowing it, needing to be reconnected with the Spirit Power I call God— or perhaps I should say being reminded of my connection. . . . it forced me to rethink the meaning of my life on earth (*Reason for Hope: A Spiritual Journey,* p. 288).

Spontaneous contemplation, or connecting to "the meaning of life on earth," may not occur often or on a regular basis. Nor does it happen unless we are open to it and ready to receive it, willing to listen to the still small voice that seems to come from within. Many times that sense of the divine presence may not be recognized for what it is, whether it is amidst the gurgling sounds of the ocean on a coral reef, in the stillness of the mountain top, the grandeur of great music played on an organ in a cathedral or in the quiet of a chapel. I have also found this encounter with the Spirit of God in the quiet of a hospital room with my son, in early morning solitude alone on beaches, in mountains and sitting in silence with soul mates in spiritual direction groups.

It might sound contradictory to say that we can prepare ourselves for spontaneity and contemplation, but I believe we can do just that. We can choose to go to a park on Saturday instead of the mall, sit at a sunny window watching birds, turn off the loud music or television for a time of quiet in the early morning (or whenever it fits into the day). We can go for a walk alone or sit on a bench and be aware of birds singing and other sounds of nature and human activity while not feeling any obligation to do anything *useful*. We can go to our favorite places and gaze at the beauty and freshness of nature, and even if we have been there many times before, we just might be touched by the finger of God in a new way.

Reflection

Thomas Kelly in his classic book, *A Testament of Devotion*, says, "Deep within us all there is an amazing inner sanctuary of the soul, a holy place, a Divine Center, a speaking Voice, to which we may continuously return." Many others have attempted to describe contemplation—but to my mind, words, though helpful, usually fall short.

Here are some definitions and descriptions of contemplation I have run across.

Contemplation is . . .

- Continually renewed immediacy (Thomas Kelly).
- Looking deeply at life as it is in the very here and now (Thich Nhat Hanh).
- A continual condition of prayerful sensitivity to what is really going on (Douglas Steere).
- The mind gazing upon the universe of God's handiwork, rapt by the divine and infinite light (Maximus the Confessor).
- The secret of Christian contemplation is that it faces us with Jesus Christ—toward our suffering world in loving service and just action (Catherine of Sienna).
- Prayer unfolding the stillness of the soul (Anonymous).
- The pure loving gaze that finds God everywhere (Brother Lawrence).
- Seeing God in everything and everything in God with completely extraordinary clearness and delicacy (Marie of the Incarnation).

- A right understanding, with true longing, absolute trust and sweet grace-giving mindfulness (Julian of Norwich).

- It is only in silence and through silence that we can interiorize what is beyond our comprehension and apprehend the design larger than ourselves (John Main).

Meditation

By the streams the birds of the air have their habitation, they sing among the branches. From your lofty abode you water the mountains; the earth is satisfied with the fruit of your work. May my meditation be pleasing to him, for I rejoice in the Lord.

Psalm 104:12, 13, 34

☞ Choose one of the above descriptions of contemplation with which you resonate. What draws you to that choice?

☞ Reflect on a moment when you have experienced a sense of closeness with God in quiet contemplation. Gerald May says of contemplation "It happens when it happens." Has that happened to you? When and where?

☞ Identify a place within your home, neighborhood or larger community within walking distance that might become your special quiet place. Can you intentionally go to this place for a time of contemplation on a regular basis? Will you?

Spiritual Direction

The great Director of Souls is the Holy Spirit.

Dom Columba Marmion

Canyon Haven Retreat Center, Montana, *August 1, 2003*

I am on a personal retreat. Yesterday I walked in the beauty of this canyon, thinking and pondering what is happening in my life. I wonder what part of that internal conversation is a projection of my own thoughts and what part is from and to God. I call it prayer when I think about my children as I walk, give thanks and express my desire to put them in God's hands. I pray that the Spirit will keep them open and that they will be open to the Spirit.

I am preparing to go to Holden Village, a retreat center in the Cascade Mountains of Washington, where I will serve the community as spiritual director for several weeks. Over the last three years I have come to an appreciation of spiritual direction. I studied group spiritual direction at the Shalem Institute and have been in spiritual direction once a month for these last three years with a Franciscan Sister named Martha Ann. Through this experience I have seen the value of spiritual direction and am aware of its helpfulness on the spiritual journey. Here in Montana, there are few trained in spiritual direction, so I have not found anyone to serve in that role yet, and I miss it.

I feel imperfectly prepared and certainly not *spiritual* enough to play this role with the individuals who will come to meet with me at Holden Village. I have had conversations about this with my hosts here at Canyon Haven, John and Jean, down-to-earth Christians who have ministered in small Montana Lutheran congregations for years. And I am reading Henri Nouwen on solitude, silence and prayer; Thelma Hall on Lectio Divina; and a book on the life of Dietrich Bonhoeffer.

There are some things that strike me about great witnesses to the faith in history, those who write so well about the spiritual journey, faithfulness and the Christ-centered life. I admire the courage of these well-known spiritual teachers. Compared to them, I feel like an impostor to call myself by the term spiritual director. They most certainly had struggles and human weaknesses but integrity is what marked their lives. They lived true to who they said they were. Many of them did not live long lives. Dietrich Bonhoeffer, of course, was executed in his thirties in a Nazi concentration camp; Martin Luther King, Jr. was still a young man when he was assassinated; and Thomas Merton died in an accident in Asia at a relatively young age. Likewise, Henri Nouwen did not live into old age. But during their lives, all of these spiritual giants were involved—reflecting, writing, praying and acting—always in transition until the end of their lives. They realized that they would never grasp all there is to know about God and spirituality. With their great capacities to inspire and articulate, they continued to communicate and touch the lives of millions through their writing and teaching until the end of their lives and beyond. But in some sense, even they fell short of describing fully the blessedness of a life of spiritual fulfillment, the beauty of union with God and the experience of a transformed life. Nouwen once wrote, "I have so many ideas I want to write about, so many books I want to read, so many skills I want to learn. . . . And so many things I want to say to others now or later, that I do not SEE that God is all around me and that I am always trying to see what is ahead, overlooking Him who is so close" (*A Genesees Diary*, p. 25).

When I mention the term spiritual direction, I usually have to explain it, especially to Protestants. A spiritual director is someone you meet with, usually once a month, to talk about your spiritual life—that is, your life in relation to God.

Lake Chelan, Washington Camp Ground, *August 9, 2003*

I had a peaceful drive from Montana and am ready to go on the boat up the lake to Holden Village. I am anxious to see what and how this works out . . . serving as spiritual director for several weeks, anxious in both the sense of being excited and anticipating the experience and also in the sense of nervousness and wondering (maybe worrying?) about how I will do in this role.

This state park is a real loser. It is crowded, dusty and noisy, though I slept surprising well on the ground. At 1:00 a.m. I awoke to a tremendous barrage

of anger: a verbal outpouring of rage by a woman against someone named
April. What a troubled and out-of-sync person. She got the "f" word into every
sentence, yelling humiliating insults at the other woman. Lord, have mercy and
give her some peace!

As always, I enjoy the boat ride up the lake and then the hairpin curves up to
Holden Village. As I move closer to the place, this time of retreat and my role as
spiritual director, the excitement within me grows. It is a happy time!

Holden Village, *August 16, 2003*

I have already been here for one week, and I am thinking about hospitality
and Christian community. Dietrich Bonhoeffer wrote a little book called *Life
Together*, which I read years ago while living in England for a year in a Christian
community called Hothorpe Hall. Bonhoeffer began that book by quoting the
words from Psalm 133:1 *How very good and pleasant it is when kindred live together
in unity!*

I was 22 years old then and exploring the world of travel and being exposed to
other cultures and languages for the first time. I look back at that time as one of
the best years of my life. During that year, my spiritual guide was Heino Laaniotz,
an Estonian displaced person who moved to England after World War II. We
had many good talks as we worked in the garden and on maintenance projects
around the old manor house that mainly served the exiled Lutheran populations
that came to England from Eastern and Western Europe after the war. It was the
first time I heard stories of great suffering and deep anguish—struggles with God
and faith. Of Haino's group of a half-dozen comrades who came to England from
Estonia after the war, Heino was the only one who was still living—most of them
had committed suicide. Heino went on to study theology and became a pastor
to the exiled Estonian Lutherans in England. He was a man of great insight, a
wisdom honed out of anguish and suffering through years in the Estonian army
in World War II and later life under communism.

Forty years, later I am in a completely different Christian community. I love
Holden Village, but as I reflect on this week I have twinges of feeling slightly out
of place. There seem to be two sub-communities here; one group is comprised of
those who come as short-term guests for a few days or a week plus those who are

here for one-to-three weeks as short-term volunteers. Then there are the long-term staff and volunteers. I am in the first group, though a bit outside of it—my niche is hard to define. I do not work regularly with a team; I don't quite feel a part of the long-term group; and I'm not a part of the camaraderie of the short-termers either. But, being an introvert, I don't mind.

I have had good conversations, some superficial and some deep, and I am thankful for these contacts. But only a few villagers have signed up for spiritual direction sessions.

Though this is a retreat center and one can find quiet and solitude here, the staff and volunteers are very busy people. They work hard and long hours to give guests a good experience, a physically and spiritually renewing experience. Though it is different, it reminds me in some ways of going to church in a new place and being greeted with a smile and then later connecting with a few soul mates with whom it is possible to have a deeper relationship. A visitor and stranger may need a bit more. A stranger feels vulnerable, alien, one who does not quite fit in. Immigrants certainly feel that alienation, and we have many immigrants here this week, literally. This is a week given to Spanish programming and Latino guests.

I suppose my main problem is that of an expectation that few groups or communities can fulfill in a short period of time. A Christian (spiritual) community is quite unique, but it takes time to form. Transience does not lend itself to deeper communication and communion. The ideal of unity in the Body of Christ does not automatically happen; we have to work at it. I found this to be true in the small groups I facilitated in spiritual direction back in Minnesota. It often takes four or five months before a deep level of trust and sharing develops. I am only here for three weeks, and then I will be on my way home.

On the way home. Custer National Forest, Montana, *August 24, 2003*

I am on a very long road trip between Washington and Minnesota. I stop and throw down my sleeping bag in this campground in Eastern Montana. It is quiet here, very quiet. The only sound I hear is that of insects and my own breathing. This is a good time to reflect on the experience of the last few weeks. I review in my mind the names and faces of all those with whom I talked—actually mostly listened to. I heard stories of struggles with faith and doubt. Some are seekers who wanted a chance to talk about the fading belief of their youth. Some are church-goers, and others say, "I believe in spirituality (or God), but I have a problem with the church." One woman lives with great pain and rejection caused by her husband; another woman feels acutely lonely and longs for spiritual companionship. Each came with questions of discernment about their future and how best to work on relationships with others and with God.

Thursday night vespers at Holden are powerful and redeeming for many. This is the service of prayers around the cross. Some of those who had earlier shared their most intimate personal and faith stories with me now came and knelt at the cross, lighting candles, a few with tears streaming down their cheeks. It was a humbling experience when people came to me and asked me to pray for them. I now remember their faces even though their names are fading. We had briefly crossed paths, sojourners in that place, quite probably the only time in our lives we will see each other, and we shared on a profound level yearnings, prayers and the grace of Christ.

The music at Holden Village was especially consoling and worshipful. One song that repeats itself in my mind and accompanies me now is from the words of Teresa de Avila:

> *Nada te turbe; nada te espante; todo se pasa. Dios no se muda, la paciancia todo lo alcanza. Quien a Dios tiene, nada le falta. Solo Dios basta.*

> *Let nothing disturb you; Let nothing make you afraid; All things pass; But God is unchanging, Patience is enough for everything. You who have God lack nothing. God alone is sufficient.*

I led both individual and group sessions at Holden. Strictly speaking, the classical form of spiritual direction is not easily practiced during a short-term stay at a retreat center. Normally it is a longer-term relationship between a director and the directee. At Holden I facilitated discussions on topics: What is Spiritual Direction? and Orientation to Group Spiritual Direction, plus various sessions on prayer.

There were also many individual sessions with guests and volunteers. In most cases the individual wanted the chance to talk to someone in a serious way about their own spiritual and prayer life. Often they shared feelings of doubt and inadequacy, but I also found that most people came with a deep desire for God and a yearning to grow in their spiritual lives.

Outside a retreat center the sessions between the director and the directee are typically held once a month for at least a year. In many cases the relationship can go on for a number of years. Here are some definitions related to spiritual direction:

> Spiritual direction is an ongoing conversation between a participant and a spiritual director in which they watch and listen together for the direction of the Spirit of God in the participant's life.

> Spiritual community is where others help me pay attention to my walk with God in community, where my desire for God is expressed and heard; my response to God is nurtured and supported. Members of the group are present with one another, supporting that place where each is alone with God.

> Intercessory prayer is rooted in listening for what God's prayer is. Group members are willing to stay in the presence of God on behalf of another.

> In group spiritual direction each individual experiences spiritual direction in the context of the group; the group becomes the spiritual director for each member. A facilitator usually is available to structure the process. The goal is to become more aware of and responsive to the presence of God in one's life. The average size of a group is three to five.

Wil Hernandez lists three types of spiritual companioning: spiritual friendship, guidance and mentoring, besides spiritual direction, which he defines as:

> . . . the structured ministry of soul care and spiritual formation in which a gifted and experienced Christian helps another person grow in relationship with and obedience to God" (*Henri Nouwen and Soul Care*, p. 19).

In my experience a spiritual direction session starts, after a moment of silence or spoken prayer, with a question not unlike that of other conversations or meetings. The spiritual director asks me something like, "Well, how goes it?" Knowing that this is a different kind of conversation than most, I know that the "it" here refers to my relationship with God and what has been happening in my spiritual life. But I cannot really talk about my spiritual life divorced from the everyday happenings in my relationship with others. So, I start to talk about what has been on my mind and what has been happening in my life.

After awhile the spiritual director asks, "And how is your relationship with God?" I respond and talk some more, and after awhile she asks, "And now, how is your relationship with God?" The conversation continues like this until this basic core question gets more and more clarified for me and I begin to see the work of the Spirit in my everyday life. In essence, she helps me recognize the God-given grace in my life.

Reflection

I took my training in group spiritual direction at the Shalem Institute for Spiritual Formation. Co-founder of Shalem Tilden Edwards says:

> The ministry of spiritual direction can be understood as the meeting of two or more people whose desire is to prayerfully listen to the movements of the Holy Spirit in all areas of a person's life (not just in their formal prayer life). It is a three-way relationship: among the true director who is the Holy Spirit, (which in the Christian tradition is the Spirit of Christ present in and among us) and the human director (who listens for the directions of the Spirit with the directee) and the directee (*Spiritual Director, Spiritual Companion: Guide to Tending the Soul*, p. 2).

Meditation

*But speaking the truth in love, we must grow up in every way
into him who is the head, into Christ.*

Ephesians 4:15

☞ Would you consider developing a relationship with a spiritual
director? What benefits might such a relationship provide for you?

☞ What traits would you seek in your spiritual director?

☞ If you have ever had a spiritual director or mentor, reflect on how
this relationship has impacted your life.

☞ If you were offered the opportunity to become someone's spiritual
companion, what personal qualities of yours do you think would be
most helpful?

The Desert

*Then Jesus was led up by the Spirit into the wilderness
to be tempted by the devil.*

Matthew: 4:1

Piura, Northern Peru, March 10, 1998

I am back in Peru to do another evaluation—a review of Heifer's program in
this country. We travel to the north and out into the desert. This is a harsh
environment for me. The Atacama Desert stretches the entire length of the
seacoast of Peru and continues for hundreds of miles south into Chile, as well.
Many pre-Colombian civilizations thrived in this desert for thousands of years
before the Spaniards arrived. The desert is so dry that cloth pieces and fabric dolls
made by people in those civilizations have been preserved intact for centuries.

Though I don't feel at home here, I try to look at what the desert offers to
the people who live in this environment. The desert does provide livelihood;
especially notable is the amazing *Algarrobo* tree, a very extensive resource here.
It provides fodder for goats and sheep, kindling for cooking and wood for
buildings. And a nice drink is made from the beans inside pods that drop from
the branches. What I like best about this tree today is the shade it gives from the
intense dry heat.

Here in Piura we saw goat, sheep and tree projects. We looked for signs that these
projects are helpful, but we must also be honest enough to see any signs that they
are not. Perhaps if we understand the desert we will come to better understand
these people and their way of life. I remind myself that the program I represent
has something to offer as a blessing, the life-giving gift of animals.

As we moved around in the desert we visited families who live on the edge of subsistence, in mud houses and with little water, money or power. These people know how to live in this desert and they strive mightily to survive and improve their lives. We looked for signs to see if what we offer, animals, training, and a few new ideas, will give strength and a small measure of hope. I certainly would not thrive here. I think I would shrivel up and die! I am tempted to shut this project down and flee, but that would be unwise and unkind.

Families we visited keep animals in large numbers, especially goats and tropical sheep. We visited the family of Don Ignacio who keeps about 150 goats in a pen. There is something here that I cannot grasp; how do you keep that many goats in such an environment?

———◆◆———

I remember the time 28 years ago, almost exactly, when one of the most destructive earthquakes of the century shook the earth about a hundred fifty miles south of here. The epicenter was out in the ocean, but the quake toppled thousands of buildings in hundreds of villages and towns. The next day I headed north from Lima over the desert with colleagues from the Lutheran Mission bringing a few medical supplies, ready to assess what we might be able to do.

Within a few days and with the support of Lutheran World Relief, I was assigned to work with Church World Service, and I had set up camp in the completely destroyed desert city of Huarmey. My headquarters for the next six months, was that tent. My self-confidence was sorely tested as I was unprepared for such a gargantuan undertaking. I hooked up with a Pentecostal pastor, Gilberto, as a co-worker. He was my spokesperson in meetings with the authorities and communities (given my still elementary command of the language) and we worked well together. I never think of Gilberto without remembering his favorite phrase—*Jehova es mi pastor; y nada me faltera!* (The Lord is my shepherd, I shall not want). He was like several other Pentecostals I have known—fervent and enthusiastic.

That was the first time I spent a significant amount of time in the desert, where adobe houses are built from the only resource people have in great quantities, dirt and sand. People have settled in the valleys along the Pacific coast of Peru wherever a river runs out of the Andean mountains and irrigation systems can be built. It was the heavy adobe blocks made from the stuff of the desert that came crashing down on whole families that Sunday afternoon. It was estimated that more than 60,000 people lost their lives in a matter of minutes.

March 15, 1998

Jesus spent most of his life in such an environment. Many spiritual masters have gone to the desert for solitude and silence, and to deepen their union with God. After his baptism, Jesus went into the desert for forty days of testing and strengthening. In the desert he was sorely tempted by demons, and he came to a fuller understanding of his inner spiritual strength and purpose. In the first centuries after Christ, people made pilgrimages to the desert seeking a word of wisdom from the desert fathers and mothers. They must have been interesting people to encounter, having lived in isolation and silence for long periods. Their words of wisdom were sometimes cryptic and hard to decipher.

My visit here does not allow for much silent time. We are actively moving from household to household to learn as much as we can in a short period of time. I leave the desert this time after only five days with more questions than answers. I have a few conclusions and recommendations, but I will sort these out later and write up my observations. What is clearer to me when I leave is that we must look beyond our first impressions to appreciate the slow and steady efforts of these families. Indeed, the desert does force them to slow down and live with scarcity, in rhythm with their environment and often with deep silence. It is the dryness of the atmosphere and the barrenness of the terrain that is most unusual for me as a person from the North. I must admit that when I am in the desert or in terrain that appears to be unchanging as far as the eye can see, I become a bit disoriented.

———————

In the desert, the landmarks are not obvious to the uninitiated. Somewhat the same disorientation happens to me in the far south of Peru, up in the high plateau, the *altiplano*. I feel limited and unable to see the whole picture as I can

84

when standing on a mountaintop. I experience a feeling of ambiguity. Doubt may seep into my previous sense of confidence. To some degree that happened to me in both of the above described experiences—the ambiguous project in the desert that I was evaluating and the immensity of the disaster I confronted in 1970.

Over the years, I have gone into many situations of acute and chronic poverty in desolate environments, attempting to help those in need on behalf of the programs I served. It is often a humbling and ambiguous experience to be in the midst of it all and I have never been able to completely empty myself or become poor myself—in the way Christ did. Yet, in looking back and evaluating projects I see that most of the time our efforts did bring a measure of both immediate relief and long-term improvements to the lives of the people we served.

Reflection

The desert can bring about some loss of confidence in our usual way of doing things, but my first encounter in the desert of Peru and the overwhelming challenges of a great earthquake also built my confidence for the many challenges that were to come in the future. In the desert, I gained some degree of maturity and skill in working with complex humanitarian emergencies that later served me well.

Wil Hernandez writes about this phenomenon in relation to the spirituality of imperfection:

> For some of us, ambiguity is intolerable because we tend to associate it with the state of being in the dark. Its unsettling effect makes us want to get away from it, in whatever form that escape takes. . . . In our spiritual life we are bound to struggle with this disturbing sense of 'unknowing' and 'unseeing', which serves as a constant reminder of our human and spiritual limitations (*Henri Nouwen: A Spirituality of Imperfection*, p. 92).

Meditation

Do not remember the former thing; or consider the things of old.
I am about to do a new thing; now it springs forth, do you not perceive it?
I will make a way in the wilderness and rivers in the desert.

Isaiah 43:18, 19

☞ In ancient times people went out to the desert to find the mystics and receive a word of wisdom that might offer them renewal. Has the desert wilderness (literally or figuratively) ever been a place of prayer, peacefulness and wisdom for you? How?

☞ Most people have experienced some periods of spiritual disorientation during their lives. If that is true for you, re-visit that time and clarify for yourself what resources helped you to grow through the experience.

☞ What gifts do you have to offer someone else who is currently experiencing a dry desert experience?

Lenten Journeys

But when you fast, put oil on your head and wash your face, so that your fasting may not be seen by others but by your Father who is in secret; and your Father who sees in secret will reward you.

Matthew 6:17

Little Rock, February, 1997

I am at home in Little Rock on Ash Wednesday. The forty-day journey of Lent is beginning and I try to prepare myself. I vow that this Lent will include fasting, prayer, study and contemplation. A good place to start is to meditate on the temptations Jesus faced in the desert. I will pray for my family that we may discern God's purpose and for my friend's adopted daughter in Bolivia. She is pregnant by rape and due to deliver in April.

In the imposition of ashes, we are reminded that we are dust and we will return to dust. I heard an agronomist once say that we are "pre-dirt," and we are certainly reminded daily that we are but sojourners here on earth for only a little while. The journey of Lent, in the words of the author whose book we are reading, *From Sacrifice to Celebration: A Lenten Journey* by Evan D Howard, is a drama—not a boring trip. I would like to make it so for me this Lent.

On this Lenten journey I am not retreating from the world. Throughout these next six weeks I will continue to be fully engaged in my work and my daily life in the world. I have many plans and will make one major trip during Lent and another journey immediately following Easter.

Friday is the day Judy and I decided to fast. I am learning, little by little. We are rather new to this practice, but it is mentioned many times in the Bible. I do not think many of my friends at work or church actually practice this discipline. But maybe they do in secret! Jesus said to put on a happy face, not a sad and unkempt one; this should be something between me and God. Don't make a big deal about it in public! Nevertheless, it becomes obvious to some when I miss meals that there is something different going on. When I say I am fasting, they don't know how to respond. I try not to bring it up, thinking that would be prideful. Am I just a little embarrassed to appear to be too religious?

Later

The forty days Jesus fasted in the wilderness has been on my mind. During the fast my senses are more on the surface. I am aware of the importance of preparation as well as the need for a stick-to-it attitude. I am also aware of a physical emptiness. However, I don't notice much discomfort from hunger, though it is there.

Sometimes I forget and break the fast, eating a snack before the 24 or 36 hours are up, and I feel like I am rushing it, cheating a bit, perhaps? And I am aware of how much meals are times of good social interaction and connection. I miss that. So fasting is not only giving up food but a withdrawal from the fellowship of the meal as well. I try just sitting up to the table with my colleagues with a glass of water in front of me, but I feel a bit out of place. I keep checking myself and wondering if I am actually more intentionally connected to God during the fast. The answer is mostly yes . . . and also sometimes no.

Holy Week

I take a look at my first attempts at fasting on Fridays during my Lenten journey. One Friday I forgot it was my fast day. I woke up in the morning and ate breakfast as usual. Once I ate lunch, and another time in the late afternoon I broke my fast with a snack, so my fast was not a complete 36-hour period. On the other hand, during this Lenten journey, I have been more conscious of prayer as I took on an attitude of looking to God in combination with the fast. As planned, I practiced silence for contemplative prayer and read Scripture every day. Judy and I have made a habit of having devotions together, reading the texts for the coming Sunday. This is not a new practice for Lent, but the texts during Lent do help to bring focus to the journey of penitence and introspection.

For centering prayer I have been using the words *Abuna de bismaya*—"Our Father in Heaven" in the original Amharic language. Reading the words of the Lord's Prayer in the original language of Jesus, I am intrigued with how the language sounds, though having little idea if I am actually pronouncing the words correctly.

Holy Week is full of worship, reflection and meditation on Christ's Passion. On Good Friday the Tenebrae service was especially rich for me.

What does the Lenten journey mean to me now? As I come to Holy Week and look back at a good journey, I feel that I should make a practice of regular fasting beyond Lent. Yet, I already know I won't do it. During Lent daily life goes on through it all as do the demands of family and work, but there is benefit in the intentionality of the Lenten journey. Fundamentally, the journey has not changed my personality. My flaws are still hard-wired into my being and I continue to be in great need of grace and forgiveness. A fast means giving up something. I realize that giving up a judgmental attitude should certainly be part of my Lenten journey and beyond.

Post-Easter

Now I am ready to leave on a trip to Peru, a place of memories. I feel anxious anticipation about what I will find there. This is not a trip I have looked forward to with much enthusiasm. But from past experience with many trips, I know that the preparation, planning, packing, saying goodbye, and getting going is a necessary effort. It is part of the journey. Once on the journey my perspective slowly changes and I start to look forward to the new venture with growing eagerness and expectancy. That is also the way of the journey through Lent. And so I felt a sense of fulfillment, completion and contentment in my soul as the journey came to an excellent climax on Easter Sunday, the day of Resurrection!

Nebaj, Guatemala, *March, 2003*

It is Lent again, and I have been trying to think about the passions of my life. This is the theme our pastor, Mike, has chosen for the mid-week Lenten services this year, and I was asked to be one of the speakers. I want to talk about mission and what I have learned from others about what it takes to be in mission, to serve the vulnerable. I have given much thought to walking with the poor, the needy, those who hunger and thirst. In fact, I wrote a book about it. But there is so much more to learn and re-learn. I have much time to consider this theme this week here in Nebaj, Guatemala, where I am with the community leaders and promoters who work with Agros.

In this remote location, I am out of touch with news of the world, but the anxiety and sadness about the U.S. government's march to war stays with me. On a personal level, I think of Judy back in the cold of Minnesota and Daniel going to radiation treatments every day. I pray for the Spirit of Jesus to be with them and all my loved ones.

I looked out the window this morning and was delighted to see the beauty of cloud-shrouded mountains high above, the same mountains we traveled over last night in the darkness. I am in the midst of the poor here, but the beauty and serenity of the natural world they inhabit in this part of Guatemala seems far removed from the great conflicts and tensions of the world.

I read this from Thomas Merton: "It is in silence and not in commotion—in solitude and not in crowds that God best likes to be revealed most intimately." Indeed, I am in a quiet place here.

Later in Guatemala City

The workshop went well, and I hope it will have some lasting impact and benefit for the participants and their communities. Manual, Rafael and I left for the city after supper even though the gas tank indicator was near empty. All the stations were already closed, so we had a tense ride up and down the mountain roads, finally stopping at a closed station on the highway about 35 kilometers from Chimaltenango. After some conversation with a couple of men parked there, they agreed to siphon off a gallon of gas from their car, which would give us a chance to get down the highway to an open station. We made it, barely, and finally got to the city and my hotel after midnight. Rafael left his family Monday morning to go to the *Ixil*. He worked long days this week on the coffee harvest and marketing project with the many coffee producing communities and was returning to his family late on Friday night. He plans to go back up again on Monday. I think that is a pretty good example of being in mission. I continue to prepare what to say in

90

April when I talk at a Lenten service and I now have some fresh material from this recent experience!

At home on the farm, *March, 2003*

At the end of my Lenten journey I am back on the farm in Minnesota on the first day of spring. Outside it is a bleak scene, gray with a few snow flurries. This is a somber and sobering week for me. President George W. Bush started a war with Iraq with a preemptive strike. The outer world reflects my inner self: feeling powerless, yet believing in God's power to change history through His people, not only through decisions and motivations of a few politicians; feeling sad, yet buoyed up by the support and solidarity of a few good friends; pensive, with too many thoughts rushing through my head, yet able to take time to listen to the Spirit in silence; empty, yet full of the Spirit of Jesus and thankful for the many encounters with people, especially the poor in Guatemala last week.

I finished my fast—a remembrance of the suffering of Jesus and the suffering of those in many places in the world where politics, economic systems and human greed keep people in poverty and misery. I saw in Guatemala that this is a daily struggle, but not one without hope.

I spoke at my home church for the Wednesday eve service—reflections on mission and the people who have inspired me by their example. There were many. Too many to remember them all, but I gave recognition to early influences right here in this church. I am sure I missed some important ones. Afterwards Evie Satren came up and said, "Your mother would have been so proud of you!" Others mentioned Mom too . . . she was much loved here. Borgany Foss, who was a close friend of Mom's and the same age said, "She would be 90 years old now, you know." I felt good for those affirmations and memories.

After the time of reflection and the look inward, it is time to move out into the world, to act and serve. This is the rhythm of the liturgical year. There is a time for introspection and renewal followed by a time for putting love into action in the world. Lent is a time to slow down: a time of prayer, fasting and meditation and a time to give attention to the spiritual life.

Reflection

Through a spiritual discipline we prevent the world from filling our lives to such an extent that there is no place left to listen. A spiritual discipline sets us free to pray or, to say it better, allows the Spirit of God to pray in us (Nouwen, *Making All Things New*, p. 68).

Meditation

Is this not the fast that I choose; to lose the bonds of injustice . . .
Is it not to share your bread with the hungry and bring the homeless
poor into your house, and when you see the naked, to cover them?

Isaiah.58:6, 7

- If you have never fasted for spiritual reasons, do you imagine you would find value in trying it? What do you imagine you would deny yourself in order to make space for God and gain personal insight into your relationship with God—food, entertainment, television or your impatience, prejudice, and stubbornness?

- If you have practiced fasting, what was that experience like for you—physically, mentally and spiritually?

- The Lenten season allows us to focus on the journey of Jesus culminating in His death. Reflect, for yourself, about the themes Lent triggers for you that you find meaningful.

- Lent also invites personal cleansing. How, for you, could Lent become a time to consider cleaning out the clutter in your life so that you could focus more on acts of human service?

PART THREE

Spirituality in Action

W E SPEND MOST OF OUR TIME in the world of work where we strive to live useful and productive lives. Most of my preparation for the career I fell into was on-the-job training, where I learned some of the skills, attitudes and knowledge necessary to help individuals, communities and organizations move toward self-initiated and sustainable development. I was and still am a generalist, not a specialist. I learned that people skills are important for this work, always starting where people are and trying to understand their reality. Skills, knowledge and attitudes such as empathy and communication are paramount. But, as Scripture says, the most important is compassion—which I learned from the teachings of the New Testament as well as from the examples of the servant lives of many of my colleagues and mentors.

Henri Nouwen wrote about compassion this way:

> It is not a bending toward the underprivileged from a privileged position; it is not a reaching out from on high to those who are less fortunate below; it is not a gesture of sympathy or pity for those who fail to make it to the upward pull. On the contrary; compassion means going directly to those people and places where suffering is most acute and building a home there (*Compassion: Reflections on the Christian Life*, p. 27).

The following section describes how spirituality intersects with and reinforces skills and attitudes needed to meet the challenges of the work of service in the real world.

Passing the Peace

Pastor: The peace of the Lord be with you always,
Congregation: *And also with you.*
*The minister and congregation may greet one another
in the name of the Lord: Peace be with you.
God's Peace be with you.*

from the Lutheran liturgy

Lima, Peru, October 19, 1997

I went to Good Shepherd Church this morning. There were only two of us
there besides the priest—oh yes, and Christ. At least we met the minimum
requirements of being "two or three gathered together in my name." This church
is in one of the richest neighborhoods of Lima and is here to serve the expatriate
residents. Most of those apparently don't feel a burning need to get out of bed to
attend the early service—at least they are not here today. We passed the peace . . .
I think we did anyway. It didn't take long.

When Jesus appeared to his disciples after His resurrection, His first words were,
"Peace be with you." What wonderful words for them to hear at that moment and
for the whole world to hear today. This is a country in need of the Peace of the
Lord. Peace to those who live with disruptions and danger and peace to those
with daily struggles and fears. The confession is part of liturgical worship and
as always in an Anglican Church, we did celebrate the Eucharist! This is what I
needed today.

What should I confess? I am humbled with the overwhelming needs and
complexity of the human situation here in Peru. I see this in my visits to the
barridadas (the slums around Lima) and confess my weakness and inability to

see solutions. But I pray for peace and wisdom, and I listened to the sermon in anticipation of words of good news or wisdom. Tomorrow I will visit poor people, but I wonder if I will be able to bring good news of peace to them. I leave the service with the feeling that the sermon didn't quite meet my expectations—but here I am being judgmental. The Word was spoken. Perhaps I did not have ears to hear it.

After church I met Shelly and Luis for brunch. Shelly is an American woman married to a Peruvian businessman. They told me the story of Luis being held hostage in the Japanese ambassador's residence for five days. This was a raid that was much in the news: a Christmas party when the MRTA—the *Tupac Aramu* Revolutionary Movement, took over the residence by force. The Tupac Aramu is one of the Marxist groups waging revolution in Peru. A more violent Maoist group called *Sendero Luminoso*, (Shining Path) believes that violence will bring about justice—certainly not a vision of peace.

The 200-plus hostages were divided into groups and separated into different rooms, and all were interrogated—a harsh and frightening experience for Luis. Fifty-six people were detained in the room where he was held—so crowded they could not all lie down at the same time—and there was only one bathroom. He was almost the last one to be released, so his anxiety level was extremely high until the very end.

Meanwhile Shelly and their two boys were living through an apprehensive and anxious vigil at home. A psychologist was brought in by the U.S. Embassy to talk with and listen to them—in fact we ran into that psychologist this morning at the coffee house. Shelly said the people of the embassy were very supportive. Later we drove by the place where this drama played out and found it was very near the house on Nicolas de Rivera where our family lived for a year in 1970. Old memories flooded in. This was a very peaceful neighborhood then!

———<>———

Being with a person and listening are as important in dramatic and dangerous situations as they are in the routine of daily life. In my past work with Lutheran World Relief and now with Heifer International in Peru, I have tried to provide a ministry of *accompaniment*—showing solidarity with those who live through repression and trauma. This is another way to pass the peace. For Shelly and Luis it was the professional, the psychologist, who had done the listening—the most important thing he could do in that circumstance. We too often forget this in daily life. It should be what the Body of Christ does for each other all the time.

The passing of the peace has a long tradition in the Christian Church. As St. Paul ends the first letter to the Corinthians, he tells the believers in that early church to *Greet one another with a holy kiss* (1Corinthians 16:20). In many churches the custom of passing the peace, either with a handshake or an embrace, has become more common in recent years. One hears a great diversity of opinions regarding this practice; some people are not used to the touching and think it breaks up the continuity of the liturgical service, and others go out of their way to make the practice a social event within the service.

Lima, Peru, *October 20, 1997*

Today Juan Flores and I went out to visit a small project in a *barriada* (slum) called Cajamarquilla. The vast slums surrounding Lima were created over the course of many years by invasions of the poor who came into the city from the impoverished countryside. Some of these *barriadas* now have populations in the hundreds of thousands. Cajamarquilla is smaller, and the project we visited assists a Pentecostal group that fled the violence of the *Sendero Luminoso* in the mountains. They were seeking peace, or at least the absence of war. They now live a very bleak and impoverished existence in small adobe huts on the sands of the great desert that surrounds Lima. I have been in many of these slums in the past, so I am not surprised by the sparse conditions. Yet a feeling of tension creeps into my gut here in the midst of this poverty. I know how little our help can do to change the basic conditions here.

We support a *cuye* (guinea pig) project with these families. *Cuyes* are raised by rural families in the *sierra* (Andean mountains) as an easily accessible source of meat protein. The families in Cajamarquilla are indigenous people from the Andes, as are almost all those who populate the *barriadas*. When you enter the dimly lit homes of *Quechua* or *Aymara* indigenous families in the rural areas of the mountains, you always hear the squeaking sounds of guinea pigs as they scurry to find cover. I have enjoyed the hospitality of many rural families in

98

Andean countries as they serve up a plate of guinea pig—a great compliment and display of generosity from their humble farmstead.

I have to agree with Juan that the most important assistance we offer here is accompaniment. If people in dire circumstances know we are walking with them, they may gain some semblance of security—maybe this is passing the peace. In addition, this project provides nutritional improvement for the families by helping them raise small animals. So there might be a greater benefit than it appears to be on the surface. The families with whom we meet, as is always true in project visits, express gratitude for the gift of these small animals. They reiterate their intention to "pass on the gift" to other families so that their neighbors might also benefit in the future. As I leave this place and return to the city, I think I have seen again the truth that God chooses what is weak in the world to humble the strong. Juan likes to use the term "passing on the solidarity"—I like passing the peace.

The Pentecostals are a pious and overtly religious people. They speak openly of faith, God's will and God's goodness. They routinely use phrases like, "*Gracias a Dios*" and "*Si Dios quiere*"—(Thanks be to God. If God's wishes. If it is the will of God). And they thank us profusely for the help we are giving them. I speak some words of encouragement and tell them how impressed we are with their efforts to work themselves out of their poverty. These words seem totally inadequate. I have been in this spot many times; what do you say when you are the visitor from outside who can barely identify with their dismal condition?

But I find that whatever I say, the words are received with appreciation and politeness. In this context we usually take our leave with the words, *Que Dios les Bendiga!*—May God Bless You! Then there are *abrazos* all around—hugs for the men and tapping on the shoulders of the women—passing the peace.

What contradictions we live with! Both the rich and the poor are targets of the violent revolution being waged by the revolutionaries in Peru, and both are affected—emotionally and spiritually. My friend Luis told me that in spite of the political turmoil and violence in Peru, the Japanese company he works for is doing very well. In one year, he sold $25 million dollars worth of products for his company in Peru. He is thankful to have escaped with his life from the clutches of the terrorists. In contrast, the families in Cajamarquilla fled from their homes to save their lives last year and ended up with nothing. This year they are hopeful that a few guinea pigs and their own determination will bring them to a better future and greater security. Their highest priority is peace!

The journey the poor have taken is one from danger to relative safety, from having little to having less, from the villages of their birth to an alien place. They may not articulate it in such terms, but I know they wish to move from scarcity to possession, from exploitation to justice and from terror to security—just as much as all human beings do.

Reflection

Henri Nouwen, in reflecting on the theme of the journey of the poor, wrote this when he was attending a seminar with Gustavo Gutierrez, the father of liberation theology:

> Gustavo's notion is that the journey of the people (the poor) is not a journey from nothing to something but from something to something. . . . The journey is not a journey of despairing people who have never seen God nor tasted freedom; rather, it is a journey of hopeful people, who know that God is with them and will lead them to a freedom of which they have already tasted the first fruits (*Gracias! A Latin American Journal*, p. 134).

What word of "good news" can we bring to the poor in Peru or anywhere we see the forces of violence, injustice and fear invading the lives of poor and rich alike? Perhaps it is simply enough to bring a listening ear, share an embrace of peace, and extend an act of kindness—like some guinea pigs or a meal with friends. For Christians in rich countries, it means raising our consciousness about the injustice of poverty and hunger, advocating for just policies and opening our wallets to support ministries that bring hope and justice to the poor.

Meditation

*Peace be to the whole community, and love with faith,
from God the Father and the Lord Jesus Christ.*

Ephesians 6:23

☞ When you pass the peace in worship, what is that experience like for you?

☞ Beyond the worship experience, how might you, in your own personal way, bring peace to those you encounter each day?

☞ What ministries that work for peace and justice can you support through donations and volunteering?

☞ When you pray for peace, do you really believe it makes a difference? How?

Presence—Vietnam Revisited

When my land has peace I shall go visiting.
I shall go visiting to villages turned into prairies.
Go visiting the forests destroyed by fire;
When my people are no longer killing each other
Everyone will go out on the street to cry out with smiles.

Vietnamese folk song by Trinh Cong Son

Ho Chi Minh City, formerly Saigon, Vietnam, November 14, 1998

I have returned to the land that changed so many lives in the 1960s—both Vietnamese and American. Most surely this includes my life. In this land many lives ended violently, but also this is where some began their lives in that decade, including our son Bret, born in Nha Trang in 1967.

I was greeted at the airport by a gentle tropical rain and a young man named Thong. On the ride by taxi into the city I recognized little. So much had changed, and I could not easily get my bearings. The first word I distinguished in the guest-house was spoken by the maid who said, *Sin Loi*—I'm sorry. I remembered enough to respond in Vietnamese—No problem and *Cam ahn co*—Thank you.

I went out to see what I could find of the old Saigon landmarks. *Tu Do* street (pronounced doo ya), famous for bar girls in the nightclubs the U.S. soldiers frequented, now has many upscale shops and restaurants. The Majestic Hotel is totally upgraded and modernized, as are the Continental and Caravelle. There are an estimated 4.5 million small Japanese motorcycles in Vietnam, and many of them are crowding the streets of Ho Chi Minh City. More impressions: Vietnamese food is such a taste delight it makes my mouth water to think about it; multiple waiters hover over their customers in restaurants; the *ao dai*, the traditional dress of Vietnamese women, is still about the most graceful female attire in the world; and there are few overweight people.

Mekong Delta, *November 16, 1998*

This is a part of the country we never ventured into in the 60s. I am now in Can Tho, the principal city of the Delta, having traveled to the south five hours along Highway One to get here. People are everywhere along the road in this densely populated part of the country, and every river and canal seems to have a new bridge. It rains constantly and feels damp all the time. I imagine the people are ever vigilant, watching the water for signs of flooding.

On an early morning walk along the river there was much to observe. A circle of young men and boys were playing a vigorous game of badminton; a group of older women were doing *Tai Chi*; a young man asked if I would take his picture with his high-tech camera; and a young woman, who said she was studying environmental studies, sat down to practice her English. Old men walked slowly by or stood and looked out at the flurry of activity on the river.

What are their stories? I wondered. What do they think about me, an *Ong My* (American)? These young people were born after the war ended in 1975, so they have no personal memories of that time, but their families almost certainly were affected by the war. No one took notice of me, the only Caucasian around this morning.

Dr. Loc (pronounced Laap), our representative in Vietnam, is an interesting man. He is a veterinarian and a professor at the university, besides running a fairly extensive Heifer program here in the Delta. His intense, almost hyper, personality contrasts with what he told me about his meditation practice, which he has been doing every day since 1976. He apparently needs less sleep than the normal person. Every night, usually from midnight to 2:00 a.m., he sits up in bed in a lotus position, faces south, breathes rhythmically, and meditates. He says he concentrates on the top of his head and draws power from the universe. He did not mention a Supreme Being or God. His enthusiasm and fast rate of speech in somewhat limited English, makes some of his explanations a bit confusing.

As the days went on I asked Loc at breakfast how his mediation went the previous night. Sometimes he said he mediated for three or more hours; yet, this did not seem to decrease his energy level as he continued through each day at high velocity. He did not sit still for long and did not match my image of a calm and peaceful Buddhist. I consider my 20 minutes of prayer each day to be puny in comparison to Loc's disciplined practice of meditation.

There is a bustling entrepreneurial atmosphere and openness everywhere. I cannot easily detect controls and constraints to freedom. There is no sense of a police state. In fact, I see little evidence of the military or police anywhere. Yet, there is much evidence of need and poverty, more of squalor and poor living conditions than of actual hunger.

We took a boat trip up the Mekong River to a cattle project to visit in the homes of five of the 37 families that have received help from this project. I am training the team to do participatory evaluation. We found that the families received considerable income from the sale of a bull calf. All are appreciative of the project, though they don't seem to know who is behind it. They probably think it is the government. The living conditions of these families are little different from what I remember of peasant households in the 1960s in other parts of the country: bamboo huts, dirt floors, sparse furniture and the most rudimentary utensils in the kitchens.

Loc's wife, Hu, works in the kind of enterprise that appears to be Vietnam's hope for the future—a shrimp processing company that exports many tons of fresh- and salt-water shrimp daily to Japan and the United States. We took a tour. The plant is super hygienic and employs 1,500 workers, most of them young women, who stand all day doing repetitive tasks on an assembly line. Their wages are higher than the average for the country, above what the rural poor can earn. This state-owned enterprise had $50 million in revenue and $2 million in profits last year.

During our several weeks in Vietnam, we saw more of this kind of industry. Some are alliances between the government and multi-national corporations, shining examples of free enterprise and capitalism! I mused about what the war to establish a communist state and workers' paradise was all about. Do any of the parties that lost so much blood and treasure in that protracted war really know what they fought for—the French, the Americans, the Vietnamese from North and South? For the victors, those now in control of the country, it was about nationalism and throwing off the yoke of colonialism. The Americans thought it was to stop communism.

Loc is doing a good job with the program in Vietnam, organizing a large network of government-employed professionals to initiate and manage projects at no cost to Heifer. He is trying to be participatory—one of our program cornerstones, but that style is really not in his nature. He delegates responsibility to people to get things done, but not in an autocratic way. He and his assistant, Thong, did an excellent job of organizing our time together with the Southeast Asia team, and we had a productive week, much appreciated by all.

Ho Chi Minh City, Sunday, November 22, 1998

Back in Saigon (can't get used to calling it Ho Chi Minh City): I took a walk and ended up at the Catholic cathedral during a Mass, one of six or seven on the schedule today. The church was full to overflowing, and I thoroughly enjoyed the choir and liturgy. I have been blessed to worship with Christians in diverse settings this year in Masses where I didn't know the languages—Greek Catholics in Ukraine, Orthodox in Albania, Roman Catholics in Poland and now with Catholics in Vietnam. I sat and meditated on words from Hebrew 12, *Therefore, since we are receiving a kingdom that cannot be shaken, let us give thanks.* I thought back to our time in Saigon 30 years ago and the many times I drove past this cathedral, but I don't think I ever attended Mass here. Christ's presence through the Catholic Church has been unshakable in Vietnam. Later I went to an English-speaking Protestant service and met people from a diversity of denominations. The Evangelical churches have been shaken up a bit more.

For example, in visits with Canadian Baptist and Mennonite missionaries, I learned that the Tin Lanh Church is operating; although in contrast to the Catholic Church, it is not legally recognized by the government. It is estimated that about one half of the churches that existed in 1975 still exist today. I asked what most missionaries do in Vietnam these days. Teach English and keep a presence, was the reply. It is not legal for them to do church work. Apparently there are many house churches—small groups of Christians who gather in homes to study, pray and worship in an inconspicuous way. There are no seminaries or church-sponsored health and service institutions. Not surprisingly, all social and medical services are carried out by the State.

I am impressed by the commitment and dedication of the Keeners who are Mennonite missionaries. They have dedicated years to learn the language, to be a presence, learn how things work and show the joy of the kingdom in little ways where and when possible. But the question still arises in my heart: "How does the Word become known here?" It is a question that stays with me for some days as we travel on to places from our past.

⇒•⇐

In 1966 Judy and I were asked by Lutheran World Relief to go to Vietnam to serve in a program called Viet Nam Christian Service (VNCS). This program was jointly supported by LWR, Church World Service (CWS) and Mennonite Central Committee (MCC). The purpose was to insert a Christian service presence into the conflict situation that was creating great suffering in the civilian population. Hundreds of thousands of people were affected. Displaced and uprooted from their traditional villages, they migrated to the cities and safer areas outside of the combat and bombing zones. MCC already had a medical and service presence in the country, and it was to their credit that they took on administering a much larger program supported by the other major Protestant denominations. I had recently earned a master of social work degree and Judy was a registered nurse, but both of us, as was true for others who went to serve in VNCS, were uninitiated and not trained for the challenges that faced us. The learning curve for all of us was steep and it turned out to be a training ground for a life of service that many continued after our time in Vietnam.

This was the first time Judy and I had encountered Mennonites, and we quickly grew to appreciate the strong service ethic of the young volunteers coming out of that church. The Mennonites, along with volunteers from the Church of the Brethren, come from a long pacifist tradition. All of the young men from these denominations serving in VNCS were in Vietnam doing alternative service, conscientious objectors to participation in war. VNCS was one of the last major relief and service programs launched by the Protestant denominations in the U.S. where large numbers of foreign staff were deployed. Of course there have been many other large relief responses since, but I doubt with as much physical presence as in Vietnam.

Over the ten-year lifespan of VNCS, hundreds of foreign volunteers and paid staff were deployed from all the mainline denominations in the U.S. as well as from Canada, Europe and other Asian countries. We joined a larger number of Vietnamese staff in dozens of project sites around the country to work in hospitals, clinics, refugee feeding centers, agriculture, social work, amputee and physical therapy projects. Wherever it was possible, our purpose was to be a healing presence amidst the suffering caused by a war that most of us did not believe to be justified, especially in view of the high human cost we witnessed.

In retrospect, the immensity of the need was far beyond our resources and capacity to meet. However, if there were ever a place where the philosophy of being a presence was played out, it was during those years in Vietnam.

In the fall of 1966, Judy and I were sent to Di Linh, a small village in the highlands of Vietnam, to start a new project that served the growing displaced population of the Ko'ho people, one of the many tribal groups in the mountainous region up and down the center of Vietnam. We were joined by Betty Theissen, a Canadian Mennonite nurse, and Lee Brumback, a Lutheran agriculturist—interestingly also a conscientious objector, which is not common among Lutherans.

The only house for rent in town was a fairly large building that had earlier served as an annex of the small hotel on the main street. It was still owned and run by a Frenchman, François, a holdover from an earlier time of colonialism. A Polish man in the village had served in the French Foreign Legion during the French war. These two, plus a Canadian missionary couple, were the only expatriates in town until we arrived. The road through Di Linh was on the route from Saigon to the beautiful and cooler city of Da Lat, a summer capitol for the French colonialists, about 50 miles to the north of us. During the war, the road south from Di Linh to Saigon was always controlled by the Viet Cong. Thus it was not possible to travel in that direction. So we were rather isolated in this picturesque village, though vulnerable to the whims of the Viet Cong and the North Vietnamese army at any time.

Ho Chi Minh City, *November 24, 1998*

Judy and Bret our son, have joined me in Vietnam as part of our commitment to bring Bret back to the place of his birth, as well as for us to see places of great emotional significance from our past. On this day we traveled from Ho Chi Minh

107

City the approximately 150 miles north to Di Linh along the central highway, a route we had never taken during our years in Vietnam. Dr. Loc insisted on being our guide and interpreter, for which we were very appreciative. As we approached Di Linh, we were astounded by the changes in the landscape. Land once sprinkled with a few tea plantations on the hillsides and rice paddies in the valleys was now completely taken over by coffee plantations. Upon entering the town, we were initially disoriented. The outdoor market was not where it had been, the two Tin Lanh churches were gone, and the hospital where Judy worked was now a school of some sort. I walked past the little building that had served as a morgue at that time, and I remembered back to a tragic day in 1967 when the outskirts of our town had been attacked by a unit of the North Vietnamese Army (NVA). The next day I stood here, looking on in dismay as a truckload of bodies, 30 or 40 *Montagnard* (tribal) soldiers was unloaded to a chorus of loudly sobbing wives, children and mothers.

We decided to go to the office of the Catholic Church to ask a few questions and get some orientation. There we were welcomed by two priests, one of whom we vaguely recognized. With reason: he was Fr. Quang, who has been serving as a priest in Di Linh since 1954! Fr. Quang said he remembered the work of our organization during the war. He said, "I have your secretary right here," and he went to the next room to call him. Out came K'krah, who as a young man had worked with us as assistant and interpreter, not a secretary. I recognized him immediately; thin and slightly hunched, his bronzed face was now etched with a few wrinkles. But it was his gentle smile that brought back memories of the mild demeanor that marked his character. This was one of those heart-stopping moments. What a delight and surprise for all of us!

After a few minutes K'krah regained a bit of his English—a bit rusty for not speaking it for 25 years—and he started mentioning names of those with whom he had worked. "I remember Jerry Aaker," he said. Judy said, "This is Jerry Aaker," as K'rah's eyes widened and we all became a bit misty-eyed. He told us of people we had known and worked with, some now dead and others still living nearby. K'bret, our yard boy and the one from whom we had thought of the name for our son, is living with his parents in his village, he said, and we remembered the one-eyed teenager who always had a smile on his face.

K'krah is now working as a catechist with the Catholic Church, providing religious instruction to his own people, the Ko'ho. I didn't even know he was a Catholic; perhaps back then he wasn't. But we had precious little time to inquire or share anything about his faith journeys.

We walked down the street to our old house, and K'rah introduced us to the current occupants, who run a restaurant and hostel there now. We were like kids in a candy shop showing Bret the place we lived before he was born. We looked into some of the rooms, but did not go into the one that had been our bedroom. That was where Ted Studebaker, one of our successors, was killed in 1971. We've heard two versions of what happened on that awful night. What is quite certain is that this was one of those terrible "mistakes" that happen in war, not a planned attack by local Viet Cong or NVA soldiers. It is clear from many accounts that Ted was much loved by local Vietnamese and K'ho people. Ted was a conscientious objector from the Church of the Brethren, serving as a volunteer, and had recently married a young Chinese woman. K'krah said he was there on the night Ted was killed. "I carried his body out of the room," he said with an emotion that he clearly could not articulate to us well in English.

Then we went to K'Jong, which had been the refugee camp outside of town where we spent much of our time. It is now an extension of Di Linh, grown into a village with its own character. It was unrecognizable to us because of the lush tropical vegetation and permanent buildings which had grown up all around. K'krah proudly introduced us to his family, a beautiful wife, his daughter and her husband and baby. We carefully took down all the names of K'krah's eight children, took pictures and promised to try to communicate. But in his situation, we found out later, postal service either is nonexistent, or the letter that we sent later from Ho Chi Minh City was intercepted. We never heard back from him.

As we left Di Linh, many thoughts and questions circulated in my head. What about the many years of missionary work our neighbors, George and Harriet Irwin, invested to build up the two Tin Lanh churches that are now torn down— one for Vietnamese and the other a vibrant tribal community? Was it worth the effort? They spent essentially their entire lives in Vietnam, spoke Vietnamese, Ko'ho, and French; and lived close to the people. What happens to the Church, the Body of Christ, when it suffers? Living through years of war and violence, political turmoil, repression and fear, the organized church has endured much. The buildings were gone but, I trust, not all the followers. I asked K'krah, "What did you do when the government changed?" He said, "I was smart man. I went into the mountains with my family to live for several years." Eventually he came back and dedicated his life to Christ through work with the Church.

<hr />

On this trip we traveled to many other parts of Vietnam; the most nostalgic journey was to Nha Trang to find the hospital where Bret was born in September, 1967. It was a fine little hospital staffed by Mennonite doctors and nurses, and it served thousands of Vietnamese patients for many years. It is no longer a hospital, but we were told it is now a rehabilitation center for ex-comrades. From what we could tell, it looked more like an old people's home. But then, the "comrades" who fought in the war on the side of the North would be old now.

As we proceeded on our travels I thought about reconciliation. In the Cao Dai Temple where a large number of men and women in white, red and gold robes chanted for long periods sitting in the lotus position four times a day, I prayed in my own way. When we visited the Cu Chi tunnels in the part of the country that had been bombed more heavily than any piece of territory in the history of warfare, I prayed. I held a prayer of sorrow in my heart at the memorial with a large bust of Ho Chi Minh at its center and three tall walls with 44,000 names of Vietnamese who had died in combat in the French and American wars. And that only counted those who died on the side of the victors—the Viet Cong and North Vietnamese— not the soldiers of the South Vietnamese army! What's more, those were the names of the fallen in only one province—Gia Dinh. We actually lived for a time on the far end of Gia Dinh which borders on what was then called Saigon. At night we frequently heard the bombing in the distance as the very ground under our house reverberated.

Reflection

I gave thanks for those of good will and their ministry of presence and prayed for K'krah and his family and his continuing witness; for the churches, Catholic and Tin Lanh; for missionaries and the Vietnamese pastors, that their witness of the past will bear fruit even today; for the doctors and nurses who served where Bret was born in their continuing ministry wherever they are; for the old people in that building now; for Loc and his wife Hu and their dedicated service to the poor; for the Mennonite and Baptist missionaries who now must find their own way to do mission; for the pedi-cab drivers who were in the South Vietnamese military and are now ostracized for having fought on the wrong side; for government leaders that they might see and know the importance of reconciliation and respect for the sacrifices of all; for Judy and me for insight and wisdom from our Vietnam sojourn; and for much more. . . . Lord in your mercy, hear our prayer.

Meditation

*By the tender mercy of God, the dawn from on high will break upon us,
to give light to those who sit in darkness and in the shadow of death,
to guide our feet into the way of peace.*

the prophecy of Zechariah in Luke 1:78, 79

- From your perspective, what is the value of simply being a presence in the midst of human need and suffering?

- What are your feelings and thoughts on pacifism as a Christian stance?

- What are your beliefs about just wars and unjust wars?

- How do you pray for those at war? Are you able to pray for your enemies?

111

Service in the Name of Christ

Lord, when was it that we saw you hungry and gave you food,
or thirsty and gave you something to drink? . . .
Truly I tell you, just as you did it to one of the least of these
who are members of my family, you did it to me.

Matthew 25:37, 40

The altiplano (high plateau) of Bolivia, *March 21, 1990*

I was somewhat disoriented as I traveled out over the high plateau of Bolivia. This is a vast plain and the landmarks are few—villages tend to look similar and the barren landscape did not change much as we sped out over this flatness, in which direction I am not even sure.

In the early morning I was granted the gift of time and quietude to walk out over the dusty road on this stark and beautiful prairie, the sun shining brilliantly, warming my body and soul. I have heard there will be a funeral today—from dust to dust. From the path I observed the daily routine of the *campesino* (peasant) households. To my way of seeing, life is harsh on the *altiplano*. Stones are gathered in mounds to clear the way for tiny plots in which quinoa, oats, barley and potatoes are grown. Whole families—men, women and children—are herding their animals out to pasture—sheep, cattle, pigs, donkeys. They all look stunted and undersized. Men are already working in the fields with primitive tools. The interaction of people with the land and the livestock made an impact on me and reminded me of my own roots and my love of rural life. But the land here is unforgiving and does not easily yield a bounty. Yesterday I heard about the desperate need for water and how limited the gains are from the projects we support here—credit, technical assistance and infrastructure.

112

I am reading about Jesus in both *The Last Temptation of Christ* by Nikos Kazantzakis and in the Gospel of Luke. Kazantzakis' narrative presents the author's imagination of what Jesus' spiritual journey was like. Jesus, too, was from a village, also a barren countryside. He knew the shepherds and tillers of the soil; he smelled the sweat and body odor of those who did hard labor; he walked on dusty roads and saw the barren land where the people toiled to produce the essentials of life. He heard the bray of the donkey in the morning. And he understood and felt the cry of the people for liberation—their hunger and thirst for the New Jerusalem. He knew temptations and the pain of death. He grew into his ministry of love and service in such a setting. How similar to life on the *altiplano*—how near Jesus is to these Aymara people! The earth here is capable of wounding people—just as humans are capable of wounding the earth. Kazantzakis wrote, "The heavens sparkled above him, while below the earth wounded him with its stones and thorns." God's creation moans with the pain of human carelessness and destruction.

March 22, 1990

Today I was with an NGO (non-governmental organization) called Qhana as we went to visit some of the development projects Lutheran World Relief supports in Aymara communities. The first stop was a village called Lanamayo. Community members came to meet us, men in brown ponchos and women wearing many-layered skirts and bowler hats. I have mixed feelings about what I saw; actually feelings of pessimism crept over me as I wondered what any development program could accomplish here. The land is extremely poor; rain is scarce; too many livestock overgraze the meager grasses covering the countryside; and the amount of land per family is only sufficient for subsistence farming. Most of the youth have already left for the cities. In the last community we visited today I asked each family head how many children they had. They answered 5, 7, 10 and the "winner"—13. I thought to myself, but didn't say—any gains to maintain families at even a subsistence level most certainly will be overcome by population growth, thus the migration from the rural highlands to the cities and lowlands. Here the indigenous families do not even participate in the money economy. They barter and try to grow enough food for their family's consumption. This year the climate is particularly harsh. We observed fields of stubby and stunted oats and barley; and the potatoes were actually all "burned up" from frost. Yet

113

these servants of the people, those who work in our partner NGOs, continue to strategize and make proposals, requesting help to carry out their programs as they stick with the people. After all, this is where they are, and they are amongst the poorest of the poor of this earth.

I slept last night in a rustic building—Qhana's center of operations—in a village called Corquimaya. It was a dark night; very cold and silent out here on the *altiplano*. It was good to snuggle down under a heavy, though scratchy, wool blanket, revisit images of the day and ponder what life is like in this environment, which is so different from my life and culture. I said a prayer to my Creator God, who the Aymara call *Pachamama*, that God's Spirit may be with these people who live so close to the earth out here on the high plateau.

It was a lonely place for me tonight, and I missed Judy and the comforts of my own home. But there was also a contentment that came over me, a feeling that no matter how hopeless I might feel, this was the place I was meant to be right now. It is an opportunity to be here in such a strange environment—the privilege of being a connection, a thread of relationship between people living in poverty on the edge of survival and the resources of my church and society in a place that is far removed from the reality of the *altiplano*. The word we are using to describe our work is accompaniment. I think of it as my ministry of service.

I know the light of day will bring a bit of optimism back to me and I will be the representative of thousands of donors in our churches who sincerely want to offer service, in the name of Christ, and hopefully bring some material improvements to the poor.

In the early morning, I awoke to the first rays of sunshine beaming through the window and the voice of a *campesino* man calling out a message across the plain. The same cry was repeated by others over and over as the message traveled across the open countryside. At breakfast I learned that this was a message about the death of a 16-year-old girl last night. There had been an accident, but the details were very vague. What happened was unclear, but it seemed that an incident happened at the local school yesterday. The teacher is implicated for having *castigado* (punished) the girl. Something about his putting on a mask of a *burro* . . . so, I wondered, did this somehow scare the girl to death? The shouted message was to call people scattered across the countryside to her funeral.

Later we went by the school. There we found that a "commission" of parents had been formed, and they were meeting with the director in the schoolyard. Needless to say, he was very defensive, denying that the death had anything to do with bad treatment at the school. If the parents wanted an official investigation of the case, they would have to go to a neighboring town of the district and ask the police to come—of course at the expense of the people asking for this service. The police simply will not do anything otherwise. As for getting a doctor to do an autopsy, they would have to go to La Paz, which is a day-long trip by bus. There they would have to hire a doctor at an exorbitant fee to come and do this service. Obviously, the case will go without a thorough investigation. Such is justice, or injustice, for the poor in Bolivia. I could see that the parents of the child were distraught, but in trying to decipher the details through translation, Aymara to Spanish, the story was very confusing.

As we left for La Paz later that afternoon, I saw the silhouette of a group of *campesino* families off in a distant field, burying the girl. They were placing the body of this young girl, who just 24 hours earlier was an active and vibrant child, into the cold and inhospitable soil of the Bolivian *altiplano*. I wondered if a priest was there to perform the funeral—"No, he would have to come from another town, and it is too far away." . . . and expensive? I wondered.

From La Paz, I journeyed on to other parts of the country. Bolivia is very diverse and is divided into three distinct geographical zones—the *altiplano*, the *valles* (valleys) and the tropical lowlands, a part of the vast Amazon basin. On this trip, I visited all three of these ecological areas, and after almost three weeks I was worn out from the exertion of traveling over some of the most primitive roads in the third world.

Lima, March 31, 1990

As I flew from La Paz to Lima on the last day of March, I reflected on these days. A hard trip, but I am glad now that I made the 12-hour journey by road down to the Beni—a low tropical jungle area about which I have heard much for years. On that trip I sat on the front passenger seat of the "mico-bus," which gave me an opportunity to view the vast panorama of plateaus and mountains, but also a full view of the sheer drop-off as we careened through the hairpin curves with precipices easily a thousand feet straight down. It was not a ride for the faint of heart with fear of heights. I suppose it is the most spectacular road I have traversed in my entire life, certainly one of the scariest.

Creation here is dramatic and people's attempts to carve into her sides to create a pathway through it have their costs. I heard several stories of vehicles having missed a curve, plunging an entire busload of passengers to their deaths in the narrow gorge below. My mind could certainly imagine it each time the wheel just under my seat came within what seemed like a foot or two from the edge.

Here are some images of the last days: thousands of settlers who migrated from the altiplano to the tropical lowlands in search of a better life by hacking out a livelihood in harsh conditions of the jungle; bulldozers tearing away trees and rocks as roads are punched into virgin lands to open up new territory of progress, hard-packed dusty roads making it often impossible to see the cars on the road ahead of us; hotel rooms with cockroaches scampering about; Antonio the campesino driver, hanging on to the steering wheel with white knuckles as we banged along on washboard-etched roads; Juan and Raul, the agriculture workers living and working in a rustic house with no electricity in an isolated jungle outpost; large stretches of jungle cleared for cattle pastures, and a seemingly relentless march of humans determined to cut down and dominate the humid tropical forests.

At every location I was hosted by local organizations and given a gracious welcome. I visited many rural projects and met the people of the villages, had discussions with dozens of project staff, and lengthy conversations over meals and on long field trips with colleagues and friends. We all have the same desire—to find the best ways to serve the poor and to work with them to create sustainable improvements in their oft-times dire conditions.

—⋙◆⋘—

There is a sense in which this kind of a journey is a metaphor for the spiritual life. On this journey, the *altiplano* is like the desert of the spiritual life—a place where the necessities and basic provisions of life are at the bare minimum. Here we need to return to simplicity. In the jungle, the ecology is complex, verdant and teeming with life, but when the foliage is stripped away, the energy of life ebbs and ecological and human communities are threatened. Here is where we need to work to preserve and conserve the natural flora and fauna, giving due respect to the ecosystem with which we should live in harmony. The spiritual life is rich with complexity, too, but with many surprises. As we look deeper we see the importance of our part in the stewardship of God's creation.

In villages and cities, one encounters every human need in its deplorable reality as the poorest of God's people struggle to survive the ravages of injustice, scarcity, and lack of the most basic services for their health and wellbeing. Here my response must be one of action and advocacy. We talk about holistic development, so sometimes I need to encourage my colleagues in this work to not only pay attention to the physical and social aspects, but also to notice the spiritual element in the people's culture.

Throughout the journey I needed orientation and guidance, or I would have surely become hopelessly lost. This is true in the spiritual life as well—the need for soul friends, spiritual directors and pastors. I also needed communications skills—Spanish at the minimum, but also experience in listening carefully to the subtleties of inter-cultural communications. One needs to understand the political, cultural and economic context and the history of a people in order to know how best to serve. And certainly I must watch for and respect the deeply spiritual nature of the indigenous people.

On my spiritual journey, I must have quiet times, and I need self-awareness so that I have patience with the pace of life of the people—the ability to just be in the midst of it all and say, "That's all right, I'm not in a hurry." The wilderness is not always a place of fear and ambiguity. It is also a place to go for perspective and to notice the mysterious.

To maintain perspective and strength for this ministry, I pulled back from the strain of the journey and was renewed by creation and by the poor themselves. Each morning, I drew from the well of Scripture and pondered the meaning of the texts in the context of the poor in Bolivia—especially the Gospel accounts of the temptations of Christ. During this trip, I started my Lenten fast—giving up the evening meal. Each time I felt the pangs of hunger and wanted to fill myself, I was more conscious of Jesus emptying himself as He faced temptations in the desert. My journal of these days was filled with notes: the mundane happenings of the days and nights, ponderings about hope and hopefulness, as well as an awareness of the grace given daily by the Spirit of Jesus in this most earthy of places.

Reflection

Henri Nouwen wrote about service to the poor:

Here we are touching the profound spiritual truth that service is an expression of the search for God and not just of the desire to bring about individual or social change. This is open to all sorts of misunderstanding, but its truth is confirmed in the lives of those for whom service is a constant and uninterrupted concern. As long as the help we offer to others is motivated primarily by the changes we may accomplish, our service cannot last long. When results do not appear, when success is absent, when we are no longer liked or praised for what we do, we lose strength and motivation to continue. When we see nothing but sad, poor, sick or miserable people who, even after our many attempts to offer help remain sad, poor, sick and miserable, then the only reasonable response is to move away in order to prevent ourselves from becoming cynical or depressed.

Radical servant-hood challenges us, while attempting persistently to overcome poverty, hunger, illness and any other form of human misery, to reveal the gentle presence of our compassionate God in the midst of our broken world (*Compassion: Reflections on the Christian Life*, pp. 31, 32).

Meditation

*Whatever your task, put yourselves into it, as done for the Lord
and not for your masters.*

Colossians 3:23

☞ Whatever your situation, what are the spiritual gifts you have to give
to those around you?

☞ What distinguishes service in the name of Christ from other kinds of
social, material or educational service?

☞ If one truly lives in the world we will encounter many levels of
human need. Have you had an experience of sincerely wanting to be
of service to people in great need but felt overwhelmed or inadequate
about how best to serve? What was that like for you?

☞ How can ministry and service to the underprivileged, the poor and
the vulnerable be a blessing to you? How can you find hope in the
face of despair?

Accompaniment

Accompaniment means a commitment to walking with—
rather than doing for.

Jerry Aaker, Partners with the Poor, 1991

Andean Region, South America, November, 1991

Three days after my father's funeral I took off on another journey. I am leading a group on a study tour to three countries in the Andean region, Bolivia, Peru and Ecuador, sponsored by the Hunger Appeal of the Evangelical Lutheran Church in America. This will bring me back to familiar territory. I have just had the great privilege of accompanying my father on the last days of his earthly journey. Now I want to make good on a commitment I had made earlier to accompany a group of hunger activists from the churches to an encounter with the poor in Latin America.

We are scheduled to visit many of the projects and some of the communities I worked with for the last four years. Our purpose is to have first-hand encounters with the poor and to motivate the tour participants—or as Roger Livdahl, the Hunger Appeal Director puts it—"put some fire in their guts" for advocating on behalf of the hungry and poor.

All summer and fall I have been working on a book about accompaniment, the approach we developed over the last decade for Lutheran World Relief's work with poor communities in the Andean region. This trip will help re-motivate me and freshen my mind with down-to-earth experiences about how best to help the poor move toward self-sustaining social and economic development. I am also interested in going deeper into the spiritual aspects of "accompaniment"—how we walk *with* people who live in poverty in a holistic way. Of course, with over 20 years of working with the poor in Latin America, trying to uphold the philosophy of a self-help, non-paternalistic and participatory approach to development, I should by now know how to define the word accompaniment. But, like the concept of spirituality—you know what it is when you see it. Putting it into words in a concise way that doesn't sound like jargon is quite difficult.

I think back on the last several years—many trips to communities in these countries, numerous meetings and farm visits, project planning, workshops, discussions and papers written. We were on a quest to do the best we could but we also wanted to learn from the experience. Thus, the book is an attempt to put it all together in a way that people who are interested in how to accompany the poor can have a resource to help them reflect on their approach.

—————

One of the most interesting and insightful people I met on that journey of inquiry was Frances O'Gorman, a nun from Brazil. One night last year in Quito, we invited her and several others to dinner at our home. We had one of those very satisfying conversations during which you feel like you are solving the problems of the world and connecting with soul mates on the same journey, talking the same language. She works with a small team in one of the *favelas* in Rio de Janiero with the poorest of the poor. She and her colleagues come close to what I would define as doing accompaniment. Over the years this team, especially Frances, became well known for their work with the slum dwellers, and she is often asked to go outside the country to talk with others about their approach. She is somewhat unique for the solid spiritual as well as social justice process she has developed. She said that her team is committed to learning from their experiences and that when any of them return from a trip outside the country, they always take time to meet and share what they have learned. The question they start with is simply: "What did you learn on your trip?" That sounds wonderfully refreshing—a contrast to the usual style of running from one project to another without taking time to reflect on what is being learned from the experience.

Frances has written a small book called *Promocion Humana* that outlines her ideas of accompanying the poor. So I asked her, "What is it we are after?" She said "transformation towards social relationships that are more just and fulfilling for all parties." Her continuum on a scale of the helping process goes from assistance and relief, to teaching and technical assistance, then participation in community development projects, and finally, to transformation. That last one is the hardest to define. It has a lot to do with accompaniment, walking with people. Its ultimate goal is empowerment and giving people the chance to have choices for their future.

November 14, 1991

On our last night together in Ecuador, the group met to ponder the question, "Where did you see the hope?" Someone said, "I saw hope in the faces of the people who have struggled to overcome great odds stacked against them."
In Bolivia we saw the people in the village of Lava Lava, *Quechua*-speaking indigenous people, proud to show us their water system where, for the first time in history, they have water piped into their yards and houses. In that country, we also saw *Aymara* Indians of the Lutheran Church who are living out the Gospel of Christ through their own culture. In the small community of Telata, the women are working to improve themselves by producing food and textiles in order to have a better life for their children in the severe climate and geography that is the altiplano. We also acknowledged our partners in local NGOs (non-government organizations), who strive year after year to accompany the poor in their struggles for dignity and daily bread.

In Ecuador, we heard pride in the voices of the people of Machinqui as they told us what they have accomplished together after an earthquake destroyed all their houses. They organized to rebuild—48 houses in total. These are now all finished, and they beam as they tell us their stories. Accompaniment means that LWR's partner here, the Rural Pastoral Development Team, will stay with these communities through disasters, relief, construction, and then the long road of building sustainable livelihoods. In Ecuador, I also saw signs of hope in the assertiveness of Carmelita, the young *Otovalan* woman who showed self-confidence as she talked about the aspirations she has for herself and for her people, especially her passion for improving the lot of women.

In Lima, we took a bus tour through some of the vast slum surrounding the city. These are called *Pueblos Jovenes* (new towns), where hundreds of thousands of rural people have migrated to the sprawling slums, living with scarcity, struggling and hoping for a better life for their children. The group was mostly silent as we passed through and looked out the bus windows at this scandal of wretched living conditions. Later we got off the bus in slum areas and visited small Lutheran congregations in Brena, Marques and Cristo Rey. This was a high point for the group. Someone later said, "What we saw through the bus window was hopelessness, but what we saw in face-to-face contact in these faith communities was full of hope."

We conversed with Pedro Velez, my colleague and friend in LWR for over four years, who continues on in the Lima office—steady, devoted and compassionate. Roger asked Pedro, "In light of all these challenges and overwhelming needs, how do you keep your faith?" Pedro just said, "By serving." Later Roger mused, "We didn't begin to tap the wisdom in him (Pedro); that well is so deep."

———◆———

I saw signs of hope in my fellow sojourners on this trip—members of my own Lutheran Church from all over America. They were pastors, writers, lay people with their hearts in the right place, with zeal to bring the story back to their congregations and make mission happen at home as well as "over there." We talked frankly about the struggles they experience in living out the tension between being leaders and servants and their desire to serve the church with all its warts and blemishes.

I read once about an abbot in a monastery who was asked, "What do you do here?" He answered, "We fall down and then we get up, and then we fall down and get up, and fall down and get up again." The walk of accompaniment is a bit like that. It means standing by those who are disadvantaged in society and being partners with those who are directly involved when we ourselves cannot. It does not mean that we can take on the experience and meaning of poverty and injustice completely ourselves. But in the action of accompaniment we step out in faith and sometimes fall down and fail.

At the end of this trip to the Andean region I jot down these thoughts. Accompaniment means . . . a humble, listening and non-judgmental attitude in the presence of the *least of these*. It is stewardship in the fullest sense—the giving of oneself for others. But I return to the question, "how?" The reality is that I know that the scope of poverty is vast, and the needs are immense; injustice seems to reign; conflicts abound; and the whole of creation is groaning for relief from our blatant disrespect for God's handiwork.

As we strive to walk in the footsteps of Jesus we start out hesitantly. Indeed it is a path we are able to tread because of the accompaniment of the Spirit. We start out on that road with small steps—of understanding, empathy and eventually participation and advocacy. We fall down—and then we get up and keep going.

Nicaragua, *May, 2007*

An image of accompaniment from Nicaragua: I visited a rural community run by one of the NGOs with whom I was working—Agros International. This organization carries out extensive community development work and is unique for taking on the issue of land redistribution. Working with a group of 30 landless families, Agros recently negotiated the purchase of a large coffee farm in the highlands of Nicaragua. These families signed a long-term agreement to work together to build a new community and life for themselves and to pay back the loan in ten years. They decided to call this new community El Eden.

Today I was with my friend, Mario Gaitan, the director of the program in Nicaragua. Mario is an exceptionally compassionate Christian person besides being competent in agriculture. But his most important gift is working with people. Walking down a dusty path in El Eden, we passed temporary houses the families had built—huts of bamboo covered by mud. Everyone was busy on this newly acquired land. This was the late, dry season—the time of hunger in poor rural villages—the time when everyone anxiously waits for the rains. Working against the odds, they hope this rainy season will be a good one. They raise their eyes upward to the light clouds beginning to appear in the western sky.

As I walked up a hill with Mario and his staff to see the water system being installed by the people of the village, we met a weary looking woman coming down the hill from a stream some distance away. On one hip was a five-gallon container of water, while in her other hand she carried another pail. Mario smiled broadly and rushed to greet her, saying "Let me carry this for you" as he lifted the heavy load from her and put it on his own shoulder. He turned around to walk back down the hill with her, and a bright smile of thankfulness crossed her face.

124

As I continued on with my companions and watched Mario carrying the water pail back to her house, he turned and called out to the rest of us, "You go on—I'll catch up with you." He soon caught up and immediately jumped into a ditch with the men who were digging a channel to lay water pipe, all the while giving them his best technical assistance and tips on how to make this project work better.

Mario literally walked with the people of that village. I have seen too many examples of directors and technicians who come to "supervise" projects while never getting their hands dirty. Most importantly Mario radiates the mutual respect and warmth in the relationship between equals—the helper and the helped. In that remote village in Nicaragua, I had just witnessed one of the best examples of servant leadership and accompaniment I have ever seen.

Reflection

Eberhard Arnold made this observation about the struggles we can encounter as we work in the face of great challenges:

> We work sometimes until we are weary and yet we see little fruit. . . . Have we been able to help a little somewhere, or have we merely affected the surface of things? What are all our efforts against the apparently indestructible powers of misery and evil?
>
> Because of the noise and activity of the struggle and the work, we often do not hear the hidden gentle sound and movement of the life that is coming into being. But here and there, at hours that are blessed, God lets us feel how he is everywhere at work and how his cause is growing and moving forward. ... Our efforts count, even though like Simeon we only stretch out our arms in the patience of faith and in loyal endurance so that we may receive the holy gift (*When the Time Was Fulfilled*, pp. 283, 285).

Meditation

I was hungry and you gave me food, I was thirsty and you gave me something to drink, I was a stranger and you welcomed me.

Matthew 25:35

☞ As you hear about all the problems and challenges that face the world today, is your basic reaction one of hope or pessimism—based on what beliefs?

☞ We all have moments when opportunities for accompaniment present themselves—when others are going through difficult times. Reflect on a situation in which you were able to offer a sense of accompaniment and support. Specifically what did you do to offer that support?

☞ What does the term accompaniment mean for you?

Good News for the Poor

. . . the resident aliens, the orphans, and the widows in your towns,
may come and eat their fill so that the Lord your God may bless you
in all the work that you undertake.

Deuteronomy 14:29

Santa Cruz, Bolivia, *April 1, 1995*

I am here to participate in an evaluation of our training program. After two days of planning and orientation in the city, we headed out to the *campo* (the field) for a week. We will spend time in the settlements of *colonos* (colonizers) who have migrated from the depleted lands in the highlands of Bolivia to the tropical jungle area to the north of here. We are scheduled to be out for a week, living in tents, and this seems a bit too much time, but I don't complain—just go with the flow.

April 4, 1995

We are in a large colonization area known as Berlin and one of the settlements simply called #45, inhabited by families who have migrated here over the last few years looking for a better life in the "promised land." It is similar to homesteading in the West when the United States was being settled by immigrants from Europe. Conditions here are at least as primitive as was the case in the pioneer days of my ancestors in the 1850s.

We divided up to visit families. Saira and I formed a team and visited the *parcela* (piece of land) occupied by beneficiaries of the cattle project, Domingo and his wife, Florencia. The house is pathetically poor—a 10 x 20 foot structure made from a few adobe blocks piled one on top of the other, a dirt floor, and some boards that leave a large gap between the top of the wall and the thatch roof.

127

Inside there are three dilapidated beds and no chairs. The children inside are as dirty as the floor. What looks like abject rural poverty on the inside contrasts with the lush tropical background surrounding them outside—and the wealth they have accumulated in the pasture on their land. About 15 years ago, they started clearing the jungle to create space for a pasture; and 12 years ago they received a couple of heifers and some training in agriculture and animal husbandry. Since then, they have slowly built up a herd of 25 head of livestock. But as is true with many people who have lived a life of extreme scarcity, they are very cautious about selling any of their cattle and using their "bank account" on luxuries like home improvement. These cattle are the only resource they have to fall back on. Illiterate and uneducated, they have only themselves to count on in case of an accident, illness or some other emergency. In fact, this is exactly what happened several years ago when a large tree Domingo was cutting fell on him. He was seriously injured and has been disabled physically and mentally ever since, leaving the burden of raising five children and running the farm to his wife.

April 8, 1995

We get a small taste of the discomforts of life in the *campo*—the small, pesky flies, mosquitoes, and chiggers whose bites cause unending scratching; smelly latrines; a makeshift water setup for washing; and the unending heat—ongoing reality for the families that live here. There are no accommodations, so we sleep in tents— and though we lie down sweaty, we arise to fresh air in the morning.

I try to remember to pray, but with the multiple tasks of personal care and preparation for the day, time has a way of slipping by without my taking time for devotions. It happens as easily here as at home. Back home, with busy daily schedules, it is easy to find excuses not to take the time to pray. It is the same wherever I am, but for me the days are more taken up with survival and maintenance here, and this is especially so for the families who live here. Jesus said he would send us a helper—the Holy Spirit—which is just what I need. I pray the Spirit will be with me, my loved ones, and the people in this place—the poor who struggle mightily for daily bread and a degree of freedom from the poverty of their past lives. I am appreciative of the team I am with. We work well together and start each day with *una refleccion Biblica*—a reflection on the Word.

Life here is indeed labor intensive—there is so much for the families to do on their *parcelas*. In normal times there is no end to the work, but these are not normal times. Rains have flooded large areas making it necessary for some of the families to evacuate their communities, and many have lost some or all of their *cosechas* (crops).

Is the work of the women valued by the men? That is one of the questions we posed to the men in the evaluation. Yet, we must watch our own behavior! When we asked some women if they would do laundry for us, they set the price at three pesos, just a few cents, to wash a pile of clothes. I said we should pay more—it is always easy to take advantage of the cheap labor of the poor. We can't criticize others for large injustices if we practice small ones ourselves.

We moved on to another community called *Nuevo Oriente*. The phrase "This is a hard life" keeps repeating in my mind. We visit with Modesto and Paulina Mamani. She would probably have been a poised and pretty woman in another setting—here she just looks tired out. I try to guess how old she is—maybe in her late 20s, but already her front teeth are rotting away. She has five living children; the youngest on her breast has an abscess on his leg. The oldest, little David, is ten or twelve. He's old enough to start doing some serious helping with chores—most likely carrying water from about a kilometer away for the two cows and a calf that consume lots of it, as well as the daily needs of the family. Modesto, thin as a rail from working in the fields in the tropical sun day after day, has suffered much from sickness over the last few years, debilitating his capacity to provide for his family. He frequently must look for day labor in a *propiedad* (a larger farm) in order to earn a few pesos to buy rice and beans. He was sick with TB and couldn't do any labor for four years; Paulina had to look for work in neighboring farms— earning 12 pesos a day, about $2.50 in U.S. dollars. Women, she says, always get a bit less than men.

Modesto could not easily respond to my question, "What is your dream for your farm five years from now?"

The things he wishes for cost too much money, he said. He has no money and little prospect to save any. The things he came up with are: a fence around an improved pasture and maybe 10 or 12 head of cattle, and especially *una noria*, a well to provide water for his animals and his family. We go out to his rice field, now ready for harvest, where he and Paulina have been working all day cutting off the heads of rice stocks with a small paring knife. They place the rice heads in bundles and tie them together. He says they have to cut "maybe two or three *arobas* today"—(about 25 lbs. in an *aroba*). This is just the beginning step. Next comes threshing out the rice by hand, then paying someone to hull it, after which he will sell a portion, probably to a middleman—plus keeping some for family consumption.

The Mamanis are putting their hope in *Jacinta*, the heifer they received from the Heifer project in Berlin exactly one year ago. She is a "pass on the gift" offspring from another heifer given to a neighbor several years ago. "*Esta embarassada*" is the first thing Modesto said about her, and indeed, she was very pregnant, as she stood in the late afternoon sun ruminating on grass she had been grazing earlier. She and the pasture are in good shape. Her first calf is promised to another family—meaning that after that commitment is met, the family will own Jacinta free and clear. She is their hope for the future.

April 9, 1995

Palm Sunday: I awaken early. It is hot in the tent, even though there is a slight breeze coming from the south—the beginning of a *surena*, (south wind) they say—the cold air that blows from the Antarctic several times a year. As I scan around the community, it looks like this day starts like all others for people here, families going about daily life and work. I do not see that much attention is given to spiritual practice here, though last night in Santa Rosa there was a small group in the Evangelical church singing *coritos*—Christian songs. I am sure that in the cities there will be large processions into the churches for Mass today, but out here in the *campo* we will carry on with our evaluation work, gathering more information and impressions. Anyway, there is no church here, so we will make do with personal and group devotions.

We finished our work and left the last community, *2 de Agosto*, at about 10:00 p.m. We drove through billowing dust for many miles on our way back to the city, arriving in Santa Cruz in the early morning. We got out, tired and dirty, just before the heavy rains, but we said to each other with a feeling of satisfaction "we completed the entire program."

On the trip back, we talked about impressions, about great injustices we observe in our work, and how we reconcile in our minds the disparities between the rich and the poor. I am reading *Full House* by the World Watch Institute, about the world's population pushing the outer edges of the ecological and natural limits of the earth. There is much to think about, especially as we have just seen a prime example of this phenomenon. It is easy to become discouraged and pessimistic, but usually, when I come out of experiences like this, having taken a close look at the lives of the poor and our efforts to help, I have an inner glow of optimism and hope. I remember the faces of Modesto and Paulina and many others we met in community meetings and on their farms. I like viewing a great sweeping analysis of the big picture, but it is only in the details of people's lives, the many little pictures and stories, that I can be renewed in spirit. I have gone to the colonization areas of Bolivia a number of times over the course of many years. It has been a fascination of mine, the notion of the movement of people to the promised land. But I always come away asking the question: What does "Blessed are the Poor" mean? What is good news to the poor here in the midst of such poverty and the struggle for a better life? I need some time to process these questions.

—⊷◆⊶—

I returned to Bolivia four months later to continue working with the staff and our partners in this program and to visit many more communities, most of which I had not been to before or had not visited for a very long time. The good news is that the national association of small cattle raisers that we started some years ago now has over 1,200 members, all of them benefitting from training, organization and live-stock. We concluded that the program has been of great economic help to hundreds of families. We saw that the highest priority of the participants was to have a "living savings account" in the form of animals out in the pasture as available emergency funds, *cuando haya necesidad especial* (whenever there is a special need) —be that money to send their children to school, medical emergencies, a death in the family or clothes. They usually do not focus on clean living conditions or an improvement in the house, such as we might prioritize from our perspective. We conclude that we need to continue to provide education on health and hygiene. And though we still see malnourished children, all the families now have milk as a source of protein.

During that trip in August, I also went to Potosi, where we visited a poultry project carried out in partnership with the local Catholic parish. We were hosted by Padre

Barabe, a Belgian priest who for over 30 years has labored in a ministry of love and service in this, one of the poorest areas in the hemisphere. I asked Lely, the Belgian nun who had accompanied this ministry all these years, what had been their vision in the beginning. She said, "It always was to stay close to the people and work on little things that they thought were important." These little things have resulted, over the years, in a secondary school for 400 students, boarding homes for boys and girls from the rural areas so they can complete their education in the town, many water and health projects, roads, irrigation, and agriculture projects, like the *pollo* (chickens) project we are now supporting with them. These are in addition to the work of training lay catechists, conducting daily Mass, and all the other ongoing pastoral work of the parish.

We had good discussions about the culture and history of Potosi and the community of Caixe D, where our project is located. Four hundred years ago, Potosi was one of the richest and largest cities in the world. The Spaniards extracted huge quantities of silver and gold from the mines in the mountain towering over Potosi and sent it back to Spain. They imported 2,000 Africans to work the mines, but these slaves soon expired in the harsh conditions and high altitude of the Bolivian Andes. Then they turned to conscripting the local inhabitants of these mountains, the Quechua Indians. Laboring under the most inhumane of conditions, many of them also died or completely lost their health. The parish carries on its ministry of word and deed with the modern descendants of these Indians, many still plagued by extreme poverty, ignorance, fear of evil spirits, and addiction to alcohol.

Reflection

Jesus repeats time after time how important it is to hear what is spoken to us. As we visit the people in these communities in Bolivia, we need to listen well to His message spoken to us through those whom God cares for in a special way. In the Gospels, Jesus talked about the poor in spirit, those who hunger both for righteousness and for food, those who are imprisoned in ignorance for lack of education, those who are humble in spirit, those who weep and suffer (my paraphrase of Luke 6:20-21).

I went to Mass in the local Catholic Church, and the Gospel reading was the parable of the sower who planted seeds in four types of soil. Father Barnabe did an admirable job of applying that story to the conditions and context the people live with here in this community of Caixe D.

It takes tremendous perseverance even to stay and live in Caixe against so many odds, such poor soil, rocky ground and lack of water to grow crops. Many migrate away, escaping to the large urban centers, but some, like Padre Barabe, Senorita Lely and their faithful helper, Freddy Hurtado, see it as the place to labor in the fields, planting seeds of God's love and doing the work of staying close to God's people. This is truly a place where the teachings of Jesus have been lived. I would say, This is Good News to the poor!

Meditation

*The Spirit of the Lord is upon me, because he has anointed me
to bring the good news to the poor. He has sent me to proclaim release
to the captives and recovery of sight to the blind,
to let the oppressed go free, and to proclaim
the year of the Lord's favor.*

Luke 4:18, 19

☞ What does good news to the poor mean?

☞ How does your faith walk intersect with people living in poverty?

☞ What are some ways you and your community of faith can walk with people who have significant material, social and spiritual needs?

☞ What organizations do you support that work to bring about a more just and hunger-free world? Why?

Peacemaking

Blessed are the peacemakers, for they will be called children of God.

Matthew 5:9

FOR MUCH OF THE 1970S AND 80S Central America was embroiled in political conflict, repression of the poor, revolutions and civil wars. This was particularly true for Nicaragua, El Salvador and Guatemala. In the midst of this turmoil, we saw the quiet and unheralded witness and work of many Central Americans to bring aid to the suffering and to speak a prophetic voice of justice and peace. Here are several examples of Christian witness that remain in the hearts and minds of many, including my own.

Managua, Nicaragua, July 19, 2005

I didn't remember until I got here that this is *dia del triumfo*—the day of the triumph of the Sandinista revolution in 1979, when the Sandinistas finally toppled the Somoza dictatorship and kicked Anastasio Somoza out of the country. What jubilation and euphoric expectations that victory unleashed. Today thousands gathered in the Plaza to hear speeches of triumph and grand promises to the masses from President Daniel Ortega.

It is good to be back in Nicaragua. I would not be able to calculate the number of trips I have made to this country—especially during the years immediately after the *triumfo* in 1979 (we lived here most of the time between 1973 and 1978). I sit and reminisce—with a cold *cerveza Victoria*—the beer of the day!

Nicaraguans are some of the most hospitable people I have encountered, and I have life-long friends here. Many of the same friends I started working with after the earthquake in 1973 are still at it; they don't give up even though Nicaragua has gone through earthquakes, great floods and hurricanes, drought, volcanic eruptions, revolution, counter-revolution and governments from the right and left who have not kept their promises. Most of the people are still poor, many living in extreme poverty, their hopes raised and dashed by politicians time after time.

━━◈◄━━

When I went to Managua after the Christmas Eve earthquake of 1972, the first person I met upon arrival was Gustavo Parajón, a Baptist doctor who, I was told, was starting to organize some leaders and churches to bring aid to the thousands of victims of the earthquake. He was certainly the right person at the right time for that situation.

We worked together for over five years, building up an organization of the churches called CEPAD, The Council of Evangelical Churches, a program that has been an immense benefit to the poor of Nicaragua ever since. Our strategy was to work with the Evangelical churches and involve grassroots Christians and pastors in relief and feeding projects. That focus eventually grew into supporting programs of reconstruction and community development all over the country. That choice meant training a large cadre of young people who joined the staff. Then we established regional committees of pastors and leaders in every part of the country, sticking with and accompanying those who do the slow but certain work of building up the capacity of the poor.

Gustavo also started a health program that served 25 rural communities by training local health promoters to treat and prevent common illnesses while he served as pastor of the First Baptist Church of Managua.

He was perhaps the most gently persuasive person I ever knew; his knowledge of Scripture was certainly on par with any theologian, and he was a peacemaker.

During the Sandinista Revolution and the war in the 1980s, CEPAD was the intermediary between the Evangelical Churches and the government. It won the respect of Nicaraguan President Ortega, who appointed Parajón as a member of the National Reconciliation Commission, together with Cardinal Miguel Obando y Bravo, former Catholic Archbishop of Managua. This was a horrifically conflictive period of open warfare between the Sandinista government and the *contras*, the counter-revolutionaries, who were supported by the U.S. government.

CEPAD's activities prompted some conservative circles to label them a communist organization working in tandem with the Soviet-backed government. As a result, CEPAD clinics became targets for attacks from contra rebels, who sought to overthrow the government, thereby placing doctors, nurses and patients at risk. But Gustavo wisely moved ahead to establish peace commissions in the most conflictive areas and brought enemies together for dialogue and conflict resolution.

While I was finishing this chapter of the book, we received this news:

> Gustavo Parajón, a medical doctor and pastor who was a leading voice for peace and justice ministry in Nicaragua for more than 40 years, died unexpectedly at his home Sunday, March 13, 2011.
>
> Parajón received many honors for his work, including the 1980 Dahlberg Peace Award from the American Baptist Churches U.S.A and the 2006 Baptist World Alliance Human Rights Award. He was awarded a Doctor of Humane Letters degree by Denison University in 1981 and the Sesquicentennial Medallion as an Outstanding Citizen of Managua during the city's 150th anniversary in 2002 (Press release from the American Baptist Church).

I would simply add that my friend Gustavo was a person of great integrity and one of the most influential Christian leaders I knew in all my years of work and travel in Latin America. His legacy is that of a compassionate leader and peacemaker and a great preacher of the Gospel. He not only preached it; he lived it!

San Salvador, *February 27, 2007*

This is the beginning of the second week of my trip to El Salvador. This morning I read passages from 2 Peter, which were full of foreboding and the consequences of sin—words worth reflecting on even if they are not uplifting. There are many who have lived in harsh conditions here in El Salvador for many decades, and still many today, suffering the ravages of oppression, war and poverty.

Today I went with my friend Sergio to visit the museum of *los martires*, the martyrs who died in the struggle and violence of the 1980s in El Salvador. Time has passed so quickly since those cruel days, but these displays keep the memory of those spiritual heroes alive in the hearts of the faithful for whom they died. Archbishop Oscar Romero was murdered in 1980 while saying Mass. Four priests were assassinated in their living quarters and four Maryknoll nuns were murdered out on the road to the airport in 1989. What terrible sins were committed then in the name of some warped sense of preserving order and combating communism.

There is a small rose garden outside the building where visitors can spend some time reflecting and praying in a peaceful place, a dramatic contrast to the violence that took place inside this building on that terrible evening when the priests were killed almost 20 years ago. We left the museum with a feeling of somberness but also of awe at the courage of some who have stood up to systems of oppression and power. The reality of these sacrifices is another cause for reflection on the meaning of suffering, peacemaking and redemption.

I decided to look up someone from my distant past, that time over 20 years ago when I accompanied the Salvadoran Lutheran Church as this small denomination ministered to thousands of people fleeing the bombing and repression in the countryside. At that time, anyone involved in giving aid, especially as they witnessed the injustices perpetrated on the population, was suspected of being a potential enemy of those in authority, especially the military.

As a result, I got a phone call one day from Bob Busche of Lutheran World Relief in New York asking me to go immediately to El Salvador because the leaders of the church were being threatened with death. In fact the young doctor on the team, Angel Ibarra, had been picked up, disappeared, and some days later found to be in prison. Two days later I was in San Salvador, and after consultations with Bishop Gomez, I headed for the prison where political prisoners were held. This was to be a kind of pastoral call, an attempt to show solidarity and help calm the frayed nerves of the Lutherans.

Indeed, my nerves were a bit on edge as I entered this foreboding institution, but the prison check-in process was not overly intrusive. I indicated whom I wanted to see, and to my surprise, the guard simply said, "go into the courtyard and look for him." There were hundreds of prisoners milling around, so it took me a few minutes of gazing across the courtyard before I saw Angel's smiling face coming toward me. We greeted each other with an *abrazo* (a hug), and we talked about how happy we were to see each other, and then Angel asked if I would like "a tour."

During the several hours we had together, Angel told me of his frightful ordeal after being picked up and disappeared for some days. During that time, he was tortured in an attempt to get him to confess that his sympathies were with the subversives. The worst treatment was when the interrogators put a bag half-filled with powder over his head for some minutes during which time he tried to hold his breath. But when he finally had to inhale, the powder was sucked into his lungs, giving him the sensation of being asphyxiated. The only thing he admitted to, he said, was that he worked with fellow Christians trying to help the refugees from the war with medical and nutritional aid.

Back in the States, a network of Lutherans was being contacted by Bob Busche at Lutheran World Relief, initiating a barrage of telegrams and letters to the U.S. Ambassador in El Salvador and to Salvadoran officials protesting the injustice of this harassment of the Lutherans in El Salvador. This strategy paid off, and Angel was released from prison within several weeks. Although the harassment continued, there were no more cases of disappearance or imprisonment of the Lutherans.

Now, over twenty years later, I finally contacted Angel by phone at an environmental organization with which he is working. He said he has lasting respiratory effects from that time of torture, but his voice was as cheerful and full of good spirits as on that day I visited him in the prison long ago. As I mused about that encounter, I realized how fortunate I have been to know some genuine peacemakers and how Angel had ministered more to me then I to him during that pastoral call.

February 28, 2007

Today we visited the community of *Nuevo Renacer* (ReBirth) where Agros is working with families who lost their land and homes in the war. Several dozen families are starting to build this community from scratch. Right now they live in harsh conditions in this hot dry season of the year. They have temporary houses built with tin sheets and are living in sauna-like conditions. The people are working hard to install a water system. This is difficult labor, digging trenches in the rocky hardpan dirt. Their sweat mixes with dust and grime on their bodies. One of the community members digging in the trenches is Yohana, who says she has nine grandchildren. Her weathered skin and stringy hair are wet with perspiration mixed with dirt, but her disposition and attitude are jovial and positive. We asked, "Where did you come from?" She told us the place and added, "Where we were during the war was much worse than this. Here we have land and hope; here we are building a community for our future." I try to empathize and realize that I need to work as hard and wisely as I can to help them make their dreams come true.

I read this morning about Abram receiving a promise from God . . . many descendants, land and hope . . . so he and his family moved forward. Funny, but a phrase comes into my mind that was said to me years ago by Jose, a friendly elderly salt of the earth, campesino (peasant) in Ecuador when I said to him, "Jose, why do you keep on working so hard at your age? Why keep up the struggle?" He replied, "*No hay nada mas que hacer!*" There is nothing else to do!

So here I am run down and tired with a cold. What could I possibly have to complain about? I vow to turn my heart and thoughts to gratitude—*no hay nada mas que hacer!* I wonder how we can enter into the suffering of Jesus. I think it is by being "with" those who suffer today, even as I realize I do not suffer the deprivations, fears and insecurities of the poor in El Salvador. But then, they live in the country of "The Savior"—El Salvador.

Reflection

John Dear, a Jesuit priest and peace activist writes:

> For many Christians, nonviolence is no longer a pious option or a political tactic. It is the key to understanding Jesus. The thing we know for sure about Jesus is that he did not kill, and he opposed violence of any kind. He rejected violence of both oppressor and oppressed. He taught a third way—active nonviolent resistance to evil. He urged his followers to love God, to love one's self, to love one's neighbors,

and most radical of all, to love even one's enemies. . . . As Dr. Martin Luther King taught, nonviolence seeks to defeat injustice, not people. It recognizes that evildoers are also victims and are not evil people. It liberates the oppressed and the oppressors. It constantly wins friendship and understanding, resulting in redemption and reconciliation, not resentment and revenge (*Living Peace: A Spirituality of Contemplation and Action*, pp. 85, 89).

Those with instant name recognition as peacemakers, those who have won international peace prizes and shown great courage and stamina, have sometimes lost their lives in this struggle. There are many others, like the hundreds of volunteers and staff members of relief and development organizations I have had the privilege to work with, those who are in the trenches day after day—they also are peacemakers.

Meditation

Doing justice leads to *shalom*, peace, and always helps us to know God better.

> *Then justice will dwell in the wilderness, and righteousness abide in the fruitful field. The effect of righteousness will be peace; and the result of righteousness, quietness and trust forever.*
>
> Isaiah 32:16, 17

☞ Reflect on a circumstance where you suffered embarrassment, hardship or rejection because of your faith? How did you handle those feelings?

☞ Has there been a time when you genuinely prayed for those you did not like—or more difficult, when you prayed for those who were your enemies? In reflection, did your prayers change your attitude and behavior toward them?

☞ Who do you admire as a peacemaker? What characteristics did he/she demonstrate that you can emulate?

☞ What do you think Jesus meant when he said, "Peace be with you?" What did peace mean to Jesus?

Other Faith Traditions

Om—Mani—Padme—Hum

A Tibetan Mantra

Cambodia, *November 12, 1997*

It felt good to be back in Southeast Asia after almost 30 years! At the airport my first impression was one of inefficiency. About 14 people were processing passports and visas as we passed the immigration desk, each having a task to do in the assembly line.

I was met by Sen Sovann, Heifer's representative in Cambodia, who would be my host and guide for the next several days. At the hotel I exchanged some money but was discouraged from changing too much. The girl at the desk said I would need mostly U.S. dollars here. I was on my way to Indonesia and made a short stop here at the request of Heifer's Asia director. He asked me to stop in Cambodia to make some observations and look at potential new opportunities for projects in this country. This was a chance to visit a country we did not travel to in the 60s when Judy and I served Lutheran World Relief in Vietnam during the war.

Phnom Penh is, as the guidebooks say, more like an overgrown village than a metropolitan city. It is rather pleasant and laidback with wide streets, not too congested, though traffic is an undisciplined mish-mash of cars and other vehicles inching forward into the intersections to gain an advantage and sneak through. The architecture is varied: French, oriental, American and nondescript—few tall, multi-storied buildings.

I have been trying to grasp the recent events in Cambodia, which was known as Kampuchea when the Khmer Rouge came to power in 1975 until 1993. It is difficult to keep all the complicated political history in my mind, the

142

acronyms and political actors, especially in the way Cambodia has been tossed about violently in the geopolitical maneuverings of the super-powers over the last 50 years. It was interesting to see a portrait of King Sihanouk and his wife on the wall of the hotel. They have been in exile in China for many years now.

Sovann was 12 years old when his family was forced into the countryside during the *killing fields*, the reign of terror of the Khmer Rouge. His father was an educated man in charge of secondary education in Phnom Penh. The family was part of the mass removal of the urban population to re-education camps in the rural areas. Forced agricultural labor was their lot. At first they survived on one bowl of rice each day. This portion was later reduced by one half. They built their own villages and suffered ravages of disease and malnutrition. For three-and-half years, the family endured suffering and deprivation. During those years, many of his mother's and father's families died. His mother's family lost 19 members—such grief as I cannot imagine. Sovann expressed pain in face of the reality that many of the next generation have already forgotten; even his younger brother does not believe it happened in the way it is described.

I think of how many times we hear the expression, "We shall never forget their sacrifice." But how, in fact, do we honor the death and sacrifices of those who have gone before? Each generation experiences anew genocide and the horrific treatment of fellow human beings by other human beings.

I read today from Mark, where Jesus talked about end times, wars and rumors of war. He said that first the Gospel must be published among all the nations. This is a Buddhist country, but I know that Christ has been here through the presence of missionaries for a long time. The French were also here, and they were Christians, but their colonial history does not speak well of publishing the Gospel.

I have only the slightest grasp of how Buddhism and Christianity intersect. I am reading "Learning True Love" by Cao Ngoc Phuong, a Vietnamese Buddhist nun who was with Tich Nhat Hanh, practicing engaged Buddhism in their country before and during the American war. What an incredible stance of compassion and justice they took! We have similar examples of the heroic living of faith in Christian history (e.g. Dietrich Bonhoeffer). True martyrs and prophets, those who actually are willing to give up their lives are exceptional people. They are given to us as standard bearers and examples, gifts to show what faith looks like when lived to the fullest. I have had the privilege of knowing a few in my life, for which I am thankful. One of those heroes for me was Gabor Sztehlo, a Hungarian Lutheran pastor during the Nazi occupation of Budapest in the 1940s. (See the chapter on *Faithful Servants*.)

I have been practicing quiet meditation as of late. I know that one of the tenets of some Buddhists is mindfulness, which to me means being aware of the self in the moment, here and now. I understand what that means mentally when I hear about it, but as a continuous practice, I am far from being mindful at all times. It is a bit akin to the "praying constantly" that St Paul wrote about in the first letter to the Thessalonians.

Before I leave Cambodia, I have a desire to visit a place where people of this country go to pray. I asked Sovann if we could visit a Buddhist temple. We had just enough time for a visit at the Royal Palace and the Pagoda of the Emerald Buddha before we went to the airport. This temple visit turned out to be more a tourist stop then a spiritual one. It is never spiritually satisfying to go to a place to observe people's prayer and worship practices. That is as true here as it is in visiting cathedrals and churches in Europe or Latin America. It is interesting how little we know about each other's faith traditions and beliefs; many spiritual tourists are traveling around the world, but the depth of understanding all too often remains shallow.

Sumatra, Indonesia, November 17, 1997

Yesterday we traveled the whole day to reach our destination. From Cambodia, I went to Singapore, where I met my good friend and colleague, Jennifer. She arrived fresh from Little Rock and was full of talk and good humor. It was good to catch up. We are extreme opposites in personality, and that is perhaps the reason we work so well together in training situations. First we boarded a ferry from Singapore to Batam Island; then we waited three hours for a plane to Pekambaru in central Sumatra; then traveled six hours overland to Buttatinggi. By the time we arrived, Jennifer had been going for 48 hours; my journey was relatively short by comparison.

Sumatra, one of the largest islands of the Indonesian archipelago, is beautiful— lush green tropical vegetation. I was last here 30 years ago, not at this same spot,

144

but on Lake Toba in central Sumatra. In 1968 Judy and I, with our toddler Bret, took a break from Vietnam and spent a week of relaxation and renewal there. That was a welcome relief from the tension of a war-weary country that had just lived through the Tet (Chinese New Year) Offensive, the beginning of the end for the American war effort.

I awoke after a restful night to a glorious day. There was bright sunlight on the clouds lying on the mountains across the valley. The good news was that it was now raining. The farmers have been burning the forests and fields in preparation for planting, covering the whole region with a blanket of smoke.

This morning I read Jesus' prayer in Gethsemane from St. Mark, *Not my will but yours,* and then the prayer of the thief on the cross, *Jesus, remember me when you come into your kingdom.*

Jennifer and I are here in Bukkatinggi because this is where Kate and her husband live and work as they direct Heifer's efforts in Indonesia. We are gathering the Heifer team from all over Asia—some are already here—to hold a team meeting and introduce them to the values-based model that Heifer has now adopted for use all over the world. They come from China, Vietnam, Cambodia, Thailand, India, Bangladesh and the Philippines. Americans and Indonesians fill out the team. In this group, there are Hindus, Buddhists, Muslims, Baha'i and Christians, and perhaps some who do not identify themselves with any faith tradition.

When we arrived, we learned that Kate's father had just died back in her hometown in New York. She decided to stay here with us until our workshop was finished rather than rush home for the funeral. By this act she gifted us with her presence. I learned that her father was a Roman Catholic and that Kate grew up in that faith tradition, but I know she is now a Baha'i. I ponder what could be said as we opened our meeting to try to give tribute and recognition to Kate for her loss and to honor her father's life in some way. Each of us is from a diverse tradition and culture, and we differ in our ways of extending love and condolences at a time of loss. This was not my strong suit, but I went off to think about it and write some notes:

> Throughout life, people come into our lives, and we come into the lives of others. This group, which is now coming into being—this community—will

exist for only a short time. Some of us are already friends and colleagues. Some new relationships will be born here, and others will grow and be nurtured. Some relationships will endure, while others will end when we leave each other in a few days. As we touch others' lives and they touch ours, we are changed in some way. We don't know what that might be—a slight change or a change of heart at a deeper level.

For most of us, our deepest and most enduring relationships are with parents, spouses, brothers, sisters, children, grandchildren, and of course, friends. Each of us, in our own way, give thanks for those who have had so much to do with giving meaning to our lives. These are the ones who modeled the values we now live by. I know that some of you have lost family and friends—I heard much of this recently in my stop in Cambodia. Our sister, Kate, is such a one—she lost her dear father just days ago. But she is honoring and serving us by being present with us these days rather than with her family. Thank you, Kate.

In my tradition we often refer to a verse from the Hebrew Scriptures at such a time as this. Psalm 121:8 reads, *The Lord will keep your going out and your coming in from this time on and forever more.* Now we will pause for some moments of silence and prayer to remember, appreciate and love, in memory of those who have recently died, and for those, like Kate, who have lost a loved one. Let us also celebrate these lives.

After I spoke these words of introduction and we observed silence, several of those gathered shared their thoughts, their condolences and recent losses in their own lives. They were surprisingly intimate in their sharing. A bonding and building of community formed in a very natural and Spirit-filled way.

Next I introduced the theme of values and used a simple question for all to respond to: Who is a person, living or dead, who is a spiritual hero for you? Someone who you could truly say influenced you and shaped the values you live by.

I often use this question in workshops and find the answers surprisingly similar across cultures. For many, the "hero" in their lives is a grandparent, a parent, a teacher or someone else from their country who demonstrated exceptional leadership and courage. Others think of well-known figures in recent history, such

146

as Gandhi, Martin Luther King or Mother Theresa. I find this question is a good entry to the topic of values and the question, "What is most important in life?" Answering this question is a way for us personally and within communities to define and name our values.

As we proceeded through the week, we found that spirituality is in numerous significant ways the most important value for many of us. One morning, Sushan from India offered to chant a Hindu prayer—and did so with a beautifully expressive voice. I was moved by the purity of it. John writes in Revelation, *He (she) who has an ear, let them hear what the Spirit says.* I thought about this. What does the Spirit say to us here, oh God Creator of us all?

As I meditated early in the mornings here in this beautiful place, I heard many sounds . . . sometimes too much noise. The quiet was interrupted by the call to prayers from the local mosque, mingled with background traffic noise. But behind and before these sounds I heard birds singing and whistling, voices in conversation and laughter, doors opening and shutting, and my own internal sacred word, *Maranatha, "Come Oh Lord."* The Spirit put questions into my mind. How can I make sense out of all this separation into many religions and cultures? God, how will you reveal yourself to us? I am listening for that, Lord, amongst the many voices, signs and sounds this week. To loosely quote Huston Smith, a pre-eminent scholar of comparative religion: Religion gives us traction to God.

The Asia team worked well together, and they thoroughly enjoyed each other. The workshop introduced them to the Cornerstones Model, the book I wrote to explain Heifer's values-based program approach. I learned again what I already knew—that just writing a book and getting it into the hands of people does not mean it will be automatically be put to use. The staff needed to experience these concepts and skills. They needed to participate, reflect and process the material in order to really learn, retain and know it. This is a lesson we know well from many settings. The research shows that when we hear something, we retain about 10 to 20 percent; if we see and hear, we retain more, but if we hear, see and practice something, we retain a much higher percentage. That certainly goes for lectures, sermons, speeches and all manner of trying to get information into the heads and hearts of people we work with.

There were "aha" moments in the workshop, so that at the end, most of the participants made plans to go back to their countries and translate the book into their languages and then train their own teams in this model. Within a year it should be available in Chinese, Thai, Cambodian, Vietnamese and Indonesian. For me it is a very satisfying result.

November 24, 1997

I am leaving today. I rose early to enjoy one more quiet but misty morning looking over the valley and tried to absorb all of what I have experienced here. We travelled around this valley on Sunday morning. As tourists we only got a glimpse of life in the villages and some historical sites, but it was enough to gain impressions of life here.

My interaction with such a diverse group from all over Asia filled me with awe, providing me a sense of fulfillment that I had the privilege of experiencing such opportunities and challenges—and this I do as my paid work!! I wrote the following prayer of gratitude:

Oh Lord, I am thankful for your bringing me here as part of my journey to learn more of you and your creation. I have been with friends and colleagues who understand and think about you, the Divine Presence, in many different ways—Baha'i, Muslims, Hindus, Buddhists and Christians. Show me yourself ever more fully, oh God. Teach me to pray in ways pleasing to you and to be your servant wherever you want me to serve you. And bring me, O Merciful God, safely back to my loved ones across the ocean. Now I pray that your Spirit will guard and guide them as well as each of these here as they return to their homes and families. Amen.

Reflection

Wil Hernandez wrote and quoted unpublished notes by Henri Nouwen:

In reflecting on his own history with God, Henri Nouwen revealed some of his most recent realizations just before he passed away. If one were to read between the lines, they contained intriguing insights into the future direction Nouwen apparently was open to exploring. . . . Some of these statements (especially the ones with allegedly universalistic undertones) are enough to make conservative Christians nervous.

"During all these years, I learned that Protestants belong as much to the church as Catholics, and that Hindus, Buddhists, and Moslems believe in God as much as Christians do; that pagans can love one another as much as believers can; that the human psyche is multidimensional; that women have a real call to ministry; that homosexual people have a unique vocation in the Christian community; that the poor people belong to the heart of the church; and that the Spirit of God blows where it wants" (*Henri Nouwen and Soul Care*, pp. 1, 2).

Meditation

For the Lord is good; his steadfast love endures forever, and his faithfulness to all generations.

Psalm 100:5

☞ What do you think about Nouwen's statement? What parts do you agree with, and what do you have difficulty with?

☞ How have your beliefs been affected by contact with people from other religions and cultures? Does this strengthen or weaken your faith?

☞ Do you believe that God's covenant with God's people includes everyone? Is the New Testament message of Jesus as the way, the truth and the life an affirmation or a problem for you?

☞ What are some ways you can respect and even pray with people of other faith traditions?

Evaluation

"Pass on the Gift"

Dan West, founder of Heifer International

Honduras, *February 1997*

I am here to facilitate an evaluation of Heifer's program, to see, observe, understand and assess what has happened to well-laid plans and projects. In the end I am expected to make some wise conclusions about what I have learned and seen. How accurate will my sight and insight be? Certainly imperfect! Essentially this is to be a participatory self-evaluation involving the staff and communities in looking at themselves and their work. I believe this is a more meaningful challenge than an external evaluation done by an objective outsider.

When I worked with Lutheran World Relief, I wrote a book on evaluation called *Looking Back and Looking Forward.* In evaluation, we look back to learn from experience. In planning, we project ourselves into the future. We fashion a vision in our attempt to make plans that are worthy of investing ourselves and our resources. In evaluation, as in all of life, we find that we cannot plan for all the unknowns that will surely cross our paths. The surprises are wonderful and sometimes awful: the serendipitous happenings, the call to respond to things greater than our plans. So often, in the midst of all our efforts, we are presented with opportunities and we either become open and ready to respond to the unexpected, or we timidly hold back.

Through the years, I have seen many lives changed by disasters, crises and other life-changing experiences. More than once, I was asked to go into emergency situations to bring aid and relief to people whose lives had come unhinged by wars, hurricanes or earthquakes. Although I didn't plan for these challenges, I am

150

glad I was able to go when called. Sometimes it seemed like the response to chaos was quite chaotic itself. So it is always worthwhile to look back afterwards and learn from the experience, making improvements for the next time.

What do I listen for, look for, and try to taste and take in to really know what has happened in communities and in the lives of the families? Again this week I see much need, poverty and hunger. My colleagues here in Honduras see this every day. From past experience here and in many countries, I know I will see, hear, smell and even have the taste of poverty in my mouth, but as always, I know I will be uplifted by seeing the spirit of poor people in the communities I visit.

I was pleased that in our introductory workshop the team ranked spirituality as the highest cornerstone present in the communities and project groups we will evaluate. We reviewed an evaluation technique that will be repeated in the communities in which each person has a chance to rank the twelve Cornerstones. Cornerstones are values and principles, such as nutrition and income, passing on the gift, gender equity and spirituality found to be important in project communities. Staff in the country programs almost always finds the Spirituality Cornerstone to be the most difficult and vague to define. They ask, "What does spirituality mean? Can you measure it?" We continue to work on the answers to these questions.

Trinidad, Honduras, February 22, 1997

Jesus was using an analogy about livestock (sheep) when He used the term "life abundant." He said, *I have come so they may have life and have it abundantly.*

Today we visited a livestock project in the area of Trinidad (Trinity). The vigorous physical exercise we got hiking up and down the steep hillsides reminded me how mountainous Honduras is—65 percent. When we arrived, I noticed many beautiful children—one in particular, a five-year-old named Kelin, is a real charmer. I took many pictures of her and her eight-year-old sister as they followed us around the village.

This group of farmers has worked with Heifer for several years, the last two or three with a cattle project. Long-term continuity is always a good sign of sustainability, and that is part of the reason for their progress. In the 1980s, they started a process of consciousness-raising with a Spanish priest working in the

151

area. Their roots and motivations seem to be spiritually solid. They know the challenges they face in their reality, and they are committed to working together as a community to face these challenges. They have lived in poverty for too many years. Their struggle is a long one, and I doubt they will ever have much material wealth. They live with little, yet life can be abundant here. They often express their faith in God and show acts of mercy by sharing and caring with their neighbor.

Earlier in the week we visited a goat project, where I must admit to some disappointment in the apparent minor improvements and the small number of families who have benefited. I tend to be somewhat hard-nosed when I am in the evaluator's role. Of course I would prefer to see dramatic improvements and big results. Then I received a lesson from the women, perhaps a lesson in humility and the importance of "small things." They related that the goat milk had been of great nutritional benefit for the children in the community's pre-school program. There is often not enough milk to go around, but these women were pleased with small and gradual improvements. The sharing of a cup of goat's milk with a neighbor's child was to be recognized as an accomplishment. I left knowing that caring and sharing was the most important result of this project.

My friend Gloria Wheeler told a story about another goat project near the Copan Ruins. This was an extremely poor community, amongst the poorest of the poor. In fact there were obvious signs of hunger and malnutrition in the children. A group of North Americans was visiting them and asking the people to tell their story. One common and somewhat cynical question people sometimes have about Heifer's program is based on the suspicion that the people will just eat the animals. Seeing that there was noticeable hunger in the community, this proposition was posed to the women, "We can see your need is very great, so why don't you just slaughter your goats so you can have some meat and feed your children?" One of the women in the project group then asked this rhetorical question, "Would you eat your children's future?"

The image of one of the campesinos, Nicolas, stayed in my mind that day as we left the highest point on the mountain. He and his wife guided us as we climbed through tick-infested grass and shrubs to see his cow and calf. A great view, but the pasture was far from the house and a source of water. This was a very poor family. The eight-year-old son who accompanied us was barely the size of my five-year-old grandchild, Leslie. We were told there were five more children back at the house.

We saw many children during the day as we visited families that had received cows or goats. Thank God they are now drinking milk and getting healthier. But looking at some of those little ones, I wondered if we hadn't arrived too late, the damage already done. Malnutrition in the early years of development is costly to human development and growth. So I have a vague feeling of frustration, even some anger that our program is so small and that the number of families served is not greater. Our slogan says, "It really works," and that is true. Oh, that we could have done more for more families. God forgive us if we (or any organization) spend more on ourselves than on the poor.

San Marcos, February 23, 1997

We arrived in San Marcos after a long afternoon high in the mountains at the community of Maraciles. We saw a very impressive project there and one that is quite sustainable. The people have been working together for over five years. Heifer's partner in this project works holistically, including health, agriculture, organization, and spirituality. Matthew 5:7 is posted on the bulletin board, *Blessed are the merciful for they will receive mercy.* But I have been thinking about malnourished children today and the opposition of the Catholic Church to birth control. I wonder: What is a greater sin, contraception or babies in the families that don't have enough resources to feed them?

February 24, 1997

We started the seven-hour trip back to Tegucigalpa and to Monte Carmelo, the center where I will stay and wrap up our work. On the way we stopped to see one last project. Perhaps it would have been better not to see it. It was disappointing. Goats have died; there is no buck for breeding; production is low; and the management is poor. Sometimes I am asked if there are any failed projects. Yes, but mostly we don't like to publish such results; though in evaluation we need to see and learn from the failed projects as well as the successful ones.

At the end of the week we had a wrap-up session with the staff and other colleagues who are familiar with Heifer and know the reality of Honduras. We heard many observations, opinions and points of view. Finally, together, we came up with realistic conclusions and recommendations. I feel good about conducting evaluation this way. It is the combined knowledge, experience and observations of all of us that brings about a solid conclusion. We all had slightly different perceptions, but in the end we could agree and see a way forward.

⬦

During 2006, I made several trips to Guatemala, working with the Presbyterian Church in Guatemala to evaluate a program that was implemented with aid that came from U.S. churches after Hurricane Mitch. We visited a community south of Quetzaltenango and a small Presbyterian congregation. These were very poor people, day laborers in the sugar cane plantations earning about $2.50 a day. I was happy to see that the help from churches has been well used here. There are new houses, latrines and health education, though the prospects for economic betterment seemed limited.

I talked with a woman named Carmen. She has ten children and is pregnant again. Sitting next to her is her 15-year-old daughter, also pregnant. These are the poorest of the poor, those who Jesus referred to as "the least of these." One of the leaders of the committee has been out of work but now had gotten a job with this program supervising the latrine-building project. He had been sick for two years with what sounded to me like a stress-related ailment. In another community, Santo Domingo, the same program is helping coffee workers who are desperately poor because world coffee prices have plummeted and these laborers are out of work on the plantations. Patricia Calin and Cruz Hernandez are two who stick in my mind. Patricia was so poor that she couldn't get together $10 to set up a stall to sell cheese, and Cruz had smashed his toe in an accident and thus had no job or income. The program of Diaconia had provided micro-loans for them to get started in small businesses.

There are times when I am tempted to question if conditions for the poor of the world are getting any better. But then I look at these small efforts and gain some confidence and comfort in seeing that indeed, something is being accomplished. Yes, the help churches send does make a difference.

Reflection

There is no exact parallel for evaluating spiritual life in the same ways we evaluate achievement of objectives and progress in the world of organizations and communities. Should we try to measure progress and achievement in our spiritual life? Perhaps not! If we put ourselves into a position of measuring spiritual growth and behavior, we fall into the danger of comparing ourselves to others, and thus, judging others. If such an effort were made, we would run the risk of living by the law and not the Gospel, and we heard much about this from Jesus. He spoke words of condemnation to those who judge others, especially those who fell into the temptation of perceiving of themselves to be better than others.

But there certainly is value in self-evaluation and reflection. We do have the capacity to learn from achievements as well as from failures and shortcomings. Martin Luther said that *reason* is God's greatest gift to humanity. He was not referring as much to knowledge and information as to wisdom. The best way to improve is to learn from experience and continue to serve as best as we can.

Meditation

Examine yourselves to see whether you are living in the faith.
Test yourselves. Do you not realize that Jesus Christ is in you?—
unless, indeed, you fail to meet the test.

2 Corinthians 13:5

☞ In program evaluations, indicators are used as measures of progress or achievement. What do you think some important indicators would be for measuring efforts to help people living in poverty?

155

☞ It may be necessary to evaluate, but also necessary to let go. What do you think about our tendency to want to evaluate what is really in God's hands?

☞ In what way do you evaluate your spiritual life?

☞ Think of a failure in your life. What did you learn from it? How has it affected your life?

Returning–Gracias!

Give thanks to him, bless his name. For the Lord is good;
his steadfast love endures forever.

Psalm 100:4b, 5

Quito, Equador, June, 1997

We lived in Ecuador for four years between 1987 and 1991. When I am asked
what is my favorite country or the best place Judy and I lived in Latin America, I
put Ecuador at the top of the list because of our good experience living there and
the wonderful people. Coming back to a place of such significance to my past
brings back feelings of familiarity. For me it is a bit dreamlike to be here. It feels
like I never left, even as I have the sense that much has changed. Can one ever
come back to a place that had special significance and expect it to be the same?

I stayed with Tom and Sandra, the couple who replaced us in the Lutheran World
Relief program when we left Ecuador six years ago. We have much in common:
knowledge of the situation, people we worked with and experience in the work of
development in the Andean region. We talked far into the night but didn't finish
all we wanted to catch up on. As I laid my weary head on the pillow, thoughts,
memories and images swirled around for a long time before sleep took over. I am
thankful to be back. I look forward to church tomorrow.

Officially both Lutheran and Episcopal, Advent/St Nicolas church meant much
to us as a faith community when we lived here. I received a warm welcome and
embraces from old friends. Lilliana and I sang a duet, "How Can I Keep from
Singing." The old Quaker hymn captures so much of the essence of the Christian
life, both the desolation and the consolation of it.

157

June 2, 1997

After a day in Quito, I moved north to Lake San Pablo in the Province of Imbaburra. I take pleasure in this place. The mountains are clear and beautiful as I walk and run along the dirt road that borders the lake. It is exhilarating to observe the early morning life of the Otovalan Indian people who populate the lakeside villages.

My friend and colleague, Susan Stewart, is leading a training of trainers workshop with the trainers from Heifer's Latin America program countries. I am grateful to be here to participate and not to have the responsibility of being in charge for a change. Susan is a good trainer, and I soak up what I can learn from her. I feel very blessed to work with Susan and be in the presence of colleagues from around Latin America, especially the indigenous people.

Let your gentleness be known to everyone. The Lord is near. Do not worry about anything, but in everything by prayer and supplications with thanksgiving let your requests be known to God. (Philippians 4:5, 6) This expresses exactly what I am going through. In our workshop we have some gentle people who tend to talk the least. Carmen, the *Indigina* from Chimborazo is here with her baby, whom she has with her all day in a blanket slung over her shoulder, nursing him, holding him in her lap. He is a joy-filled and happy baby, having all his needs met and seldom fussing or crying. I pray that Carmen's desires for her children and her people will become real as far into the future as the world exists.

June 6, 1997

At 6:00 o'clock this morning the mountains across the lake were cloud covered. I found a good place to sit and watch the dawning of the day, a place to gaze, contemplate and practice quietness. I enjoy these moments, knowing that this day, as all others, will soon pass and become a dim memory. I read Romans 8:26: *Likewise the Spirit helps us in our weakness; for we do not know how to pray as we ought, but that very Spirit intercedes with sighs too deep for words.* Knowing this lifts a burden from my shoulders. If only we could understand that in prayer we often don't need words! We can be still and breathe in the Divine Presence. The Spirit of God knows my prayer and desires, even if left unspoken!

I am with the salt of the earth, those who truly are interested in making their communities a better place to live. As a trainer, I may have something to offer to others, but we all have much to learn from each other's life experiences. I try to learn the lesson of kindness and gentleness from the indigenous people of Latin America, realizing how much baggage from my own culture I have to overcome.

June 7, 1997

We left Lake San Pablo and went to the market in Otovalo for some quick shopping. This is one of the most famous Indian markets in Latin America. This traditional *feria* is where tourists flock on Saturdays—a veritable feast of color, sounds and smells. The Otovalans dress in traditional clothing—especially the women. The men wear white trousers, distinctive sandals and their trademark black wide-brimmed hats. I have seen Otovalans selling their weavings and wares in the squares and streets of cities around the world—as widespread as Honolulu, Warsaw and Paris. They play Andean folk music on their *charrangos*, flutes and drums—music that penetrates to my core. I have a feeling of great contentment just to be here.

Though I no longer feel compelled to buy weavings or souvenirs when I travel, I must admit I still find joy to be in places of commerce that are not totally predictable, monotonously the same from city to city as in the U.S. When you come into a shopping center in any city in the U.S. you see the same box stores and brand names as in any other city; regional and local differences have been erased as we have become a homogenized culture.

Continuing our journey, we traveled high into the sierra in the Province of Cayumbe to visit indigenous families. This region is part of the Andean *cordillera* where agriculture is risky because of the cold climate and high altitude. We visited a project that is working to help families increase production on their small *fincas* (farms) in a sustainable and environmentally friendly way. We spent some time with Cesar who has about one hectare (1.6 acres) of land and is using some of the techniques being introduced by the project. He is proud to show us what he is doing and how the project is helping his family. His is undoubtedly a poor family. An American member of our group, who had joined us for this field trip, commented, "They do have a TV and a CD player." There seems to be an implication that if poor people acquire such consumer items, they must not really be poor, maybe not worthy of our help?

Jesus talked to his disciples about the Kingdom of God when he was asked by the rich man, *"Good teacher, what must I do to inherit eternal life?"* (Mark 10:17). This is one of the more difficult sayings of Jesus, and we read that the man went away sad. Jesus looked straight into his eyes with love when He told this man to give away all he had to the poor and then come and follow him.

We looked right into the reality of the Ecuadoran economic system from a high point on the mountain. From here we could see vast areas covered with greenhouses in the valley below. These are highly capital-intensive flower-growing operations with heavy use of pesticides. Exporting flowers is a very profitable business. These operations are owned by wealthy business people from Quito or abroad, or they might be financed with laundered drug money from Colombia.

During the workshop, Paco and Carman presented a socio-drama demonstrating the effects on the lives of those who work in the greenhouses as contrasted to those who profit from this export business. The rich reap quick and handsome profits from their investments in flower farms, but the results for the *campesinos* who provide cheap labor is sickness and insecurity. As land values increase, small farmers cannot stay on the land and must choose to either work as peons for the rich in these greenhouses or migrate to the cities in search of jobs.

—————✥•✥—————

Do I have an overly romanticized notion of indigenous cultures and peoples? I don't think so. For many years, I have had the privilege of innumerable visits to their communities and have been with people of many ethnic groups on their farms and in their homes in the Andean region—Ecuador, Peru, Bolivia and Chile. When I stop to remember those visits, I think about the spiritual values they have shared with me. Two words come to mind—gratitude and hospitality.

In their community meetings and in conversation, the words *"gracias a Dios"* (thanks be to God) are peppered throughout. And on numerous occasions they have invited our team into their homes to share a meal, often potatoes, beans, and *cuye* (guinea pig). Once in Bolivia, I was on a whirlwind visit to several projects in a single day and was invited to seven different meals, all with generous helpings of potatoes, but the last one of the day included guinea pig, eggs and soup, as well. I was well fed that day, to say the least!

June 9, 1997

We proceeded south to Chimborazo, the province named for the highest and most spectacular volcano in the chain that runs the length of Ecuador from north to south. It was a glorious day with bright sunshine on the snow-covered mountain and people in colorful ponchos gathered in their communities. We talked and laughed with these humble, down-to-earth people. They showed us their accomplishments with obvious pride.

I lift up my eyes to the hills—from where will my help come? Psalm 121 is Judy's favorite Psalm and one of mine, too. I have climbed onto mountains in many countries and read those verses for my devotions.

Here we saw dramatic scenery and views, great vistas, but most importantly we saw the impact of animal projects in families. In one village a group of *campesinos* (literally people of the fields) was working to start a dairy at an altitude of about 12,000 feet. Emotions welled up as I heard Jose, their leader, articulate their vision and hope for the future. But it was a single woman, Rosario, who hosted us during our visit to her small organic farm who was the most impressive.

We write and talk a lot in our profession about sustainable farming and diversity. Rosario's mini-farm provides a good example of how it can work. She had guinea pigs, cows, honeybees, and many types of crops and vegetables. We were invited to eat the fruits of her labor at her table: several types of potatoes, *havas* (like a lima bean), homemade cheese, honey, bread and chicken. It was a magnificent setting in which to enjoy food, companionship, conversation and lots of humor. We bowed our heads and gave thanks, a common practice in Evangelical homes here in the Andes.

We exchanged ideas and talked about their reality; to me it was a transformative, though fleeting moment. We had seen much, and now I think we understood more, not completely, but it is in moments like this that I know that we are all God's children, that we are all interrelated and that this work I have given so much of my life to is worth the effort. I am thankful for generous donors in the churches in the North who support this work.

When Jesus appeared to the disciples after his resurrection he asked, *Have you anything here to eat?* and they shared food together. He continued to talk to them and *opened their minds to understand the Scriptures.* That was a moment when everything made sense and came together in a way they could understand and finally know what His message and life were all about. At this moment I feel a similar clarity. What great love I have for Ecuador! Before I ended this trip, I saw more old friends and visited the art gallery of Guayasamin, one of Ecuador's most famous artists. I delighted in the ambiance and foods one more time in the company of friends, especially thankful for the chance to see Eduardo Sotomayor, whom I met when I first visited Ecuador 20 years ago. He continues to be one of my heroes and a truly self-actualized man. He and his wife, Nancy, have a dairy farm outside of Quito. It was again an inspiration for me to visit that place and see that he has fulfilled his vision and done well with the land and with his life.

Reflection

The *indigenes* (Indian people) are an intricate part of the soul of Latin America, the descendants of the people who were here first. Henri Nouwen wrote at the end of his six-month sojourn in Latin America, a time he spent mostly with the poor:

> A treasure lies hidden in the soul of Latin America, a spiritual treasure to be recognized as a gift for us who live in the illusion of power and self-control. It is a treasure of gratitude that can help us break through the walls of our individual and collective self-righteousness and can prevent us from destroying ourselves and our planet in the futile attempt to hold onto what we consider our own (*Gracias! A Latin American Journal*, p. 188).

And so it was with my experience of working in Latin America. When I worked for too long in the office at headquarters with reports and administrative duties, I always felt the need to get out to the field to be renewed and refreshed by being with the rural families with whom we worked in partnership. It was the spirit of caring and sharing that inspired me the most. I found that passing on the gift was embedded deeply in every culture in which I worked during my long career; this was especially true with the rural poor. This is why I remain hopeful and grateful—my reason for saying *Gracias!* to all the people with whom I had the privilege to serve for so many years.

Meditation

. . . and great grace was upon them all. There was not a needy person among them, for as many as owned lands or houses sold them and brought the proceeds of what was sold. They laid it at the apostles' feet, and it was distributed to each as any had need.

Acts 4:33b–35

☞ Where do you feel most at home? Name the places you return to that make you feel grateful and at home.

☞ Whether or not you have personally interacted with indigenous people, you probably have an image or impression—what is your reaction to this description of the indigenous people of Ecuador?

☞ What is the strongest emotion you experience when you return to a place you have lived before and find it changed?

☞ What are you most grateful for right now?

No ONE CAN CLAIM TO BE A SELF-MADE PERSON. Indeed, we owe an immense debt of gratitude to individuals, opportunities and circumstances that we encounter on our journey through life. On the surface, it would seem that many of these encounters simply happen by chance. Then we think back and realize how providential it was that these people and these learning moments touched our lives, even those that revealed to us something of our own weaknesses. Some, like parents, teachers and pastors are sources of nurture and formation over long periods of time. Other experiences and people touch our lives ever so briefly, often leaving us with a witness of courage or giving us lessons in hospitality, humor and compassion.

These encounters become heartfelt memories that reappear in our consciousness at unexpected times. Here are eight such encounters out of myriad others in the course of my journey.

Waiting for the Will of God

They also serve who only stand and wait.

John Milton

Huehuetenango, Guatemala, December, 1995

High on the Cuchumatane plateau, I trekked on a trail up the steep mountainside and through pastures and fields to visit farms and homes of the Indian families who participate in a sheep project that has been of much benefit in this area. Walking along a path through a small meadow, I came upon an old woman sitting on a stone wall. Her deeply wrinkled and leathery brown face displayed the effects of many years exposure to the direct sun of this high altitude.

"Buenas días, Señora, Como está usted?" "Good morning, madam, how are you?" I asked.

She smiled, showing her few remaining teeth. *"Buenas días, señor! Estoy esperando la voluntad de Dios!"* "Good morning, sir. I am waiting for the will of God," she replied.

I was curious about this greeting and stopped to chat. She told me that she lives alone. "My husband died three years ago, and I have no one to take care of me now."

"What about your children?"

"I have none," she said. "I live up there," as she pointed up the steep slope behind me, "on the other side of that crest."

She carried a piece of kindling wood and a small bag of food. She told me that she was out looking for food, and I supposed that this old widow went around to her neighbors each day asking for help in her old age.

As she spoke about herself and her life, tears welled up in her eyes. "I am 83 years old, and I'm waiting for the will of God," she repeated. In Spanish the word *esperar* means both to wait and to expect. I wondered for a moment if she was actually expecting to be called by God that very day—or perhaps was just sitting there in the sunshine wanting to go to heaven soon.

Then she looked right at me and said, *"Dios es Grande!"*

I agreed—"Yes, God is Great." I felt comforted and assured that the Spirit was right there hearing her real and sincere supplication to God—to take her to be at God's side—or just waiting to see what was God's will for her that day.

I was warmed and touched by this brief and poignant encounter on the path that day. Was it because her tears were so authentic and not intended to solicit my pity? She was not asking anything of me—not begging or preying on my guilt and asking for sympathy. No, instead she was giving something to me—something deep within her—a simple and primitive *campesina* faith in the goodness of God. And I took even more than that gift away with me—I took an image. I asked her if I could take her picture, expecting the usual shy and embarrassed response of an indigenous woman. But no—she looked straight at me, though I was not sure her eyes could perceive my image clearly. *"Bueno—Tal vez!"* she said, as if to say, "Good! Maybe that's a good idea!" It was a strong and positive response, so we connected through the lens of the camera for a few brief seconds, and after some minutes I bid farewell.

"May God bless you," was the only thing I could say, to which she responded—*"Gracias."* As I walked on up the path, I thought about waiting for the will of God in my own life, thankful for her testimony, a reminder to me.

⇒◆⇐

The old Mayan woman had shown me her faith that morning, and I am sure I was more enriched by her than she was by me in that chance encounter on a cool December morning. After all, it is Advent—and we are, indeed, waiting for the will of God!

When I am on a trip, I am not always on the move. There are many pauses and stops along the way. Sometimes I become impatient with the pace. I found this to be especially true in Latin America with regard to time. I learned that a community meeting set for 9:00 a.m. would not necessarily begin at that hour. Arriving at the agreed upon time, often meant we could expect to wait for maybe an hour for everyone to arrive. However, that was not considered to be wasted time, but rather a time to look around, greet everyone as they showed up, and get to know something about the place and the people. Politeness and relationships are more highly valued than promptness and the achievement of an agenda.

In the same way, the spiritual journey is not one of simply ticking off a list of achievements—an activity of the mind in which I strive to know as much *about* God and His purposes as possible. A more constructive use of time may be to do what Jesus asked his disciples to do in the midst of a severe crisis. In the garden of Gethsemane, Jesus asked Peter, James and John to watch and wait. They went to a place called Gethsemane; and he said to his disciples, *Sit here while I pray* (Mark 14:32).

This was not easy for them; nor is it for me. But the prayer of waiting for the will of God may be just that—sitting still in the presence of God, allowing the Spirit of Jesus to pray within me—watching for the will of God.

Reflection

In writing about waiting prayer, Sue Monk Kidd said:

> [Waiting prayer] has little to do with petition and intercession and getting God to fix things. . . . We place ourselves in postures of the heart, in the stillness that enables us to become aware of what God is doing so that we can gradually say yes to it with our whole being. . . . Attentiveness is vital to waiting. The word wait comes from a root word meaning "to watch." Originally to wait meant to apply attentiveness or watchfulness throughout a period of time and was a highly regarded experience. To wait on God meant to watch keenly for God's coming. Watchers and waiters were nearly synonymous.

Unfortunately, much of this meaning has been emptied out of our experience of waiting. These days, the idea of waiting doesn't conjure up the idea of being tuned in as much as it does the idea of being turned out. We denigrate it to idling (*When the Heart Waits*, pp 129, 130).

Meditation

I wait for the Lord, my soul waits, and in his word I hope;
my soul waits for the Lord more than those who watch for the morning,
more than those who watch for the morning.

Psalm 130:5, 6

☞ Generally, how do you emotionally handle an experience that involves waiting?

☞ What do you think the old woman in this story meant by "waiting for the will of God?"

☞ Reflect on and write about one of your own experiences of waiting and watching for the will of God for yourself or another person.

After Easter

If Christ is raised, nothing else matters.
If Christ is not raised, nothing matters.

Jaroslov Pelikan—words uttered shortly before his death

Tirana, Albania, *April 18, 1998*

Holy week and Easter have passed, and I have again left my home and family, this time to come east to Albania and Romania. I am making this trip as a part of my responsibilities as interim Heifer International program director for Central and Eastern Europe.

What an exhausting, exhilarating and awe-inspiring time Lent and Easter was for me this year! I was more aware of and attentive to prayer and fasting than before; no meat for all of Lent, and last week I did a partial fast on three different days. This put me in touch with a more contemplative life; though I am still not consistent with my prayers. I keep shorter periods of silence, not the 20 minutes prescribed by those who practice centering prayer. I recognize my penchant for words and images. Thus, I have settled more on *lectio divina* as a way to pray the Scriptures.

Leslie, who is now six years old, was a joyful part of our Holy Week. On Good Friday, we were at the Tenebrae service, which was well done by Faith Lutheran's choir again this year. As the music set the mood and the lights were dimmed Leslie started to "journal" on a small note pad, asking for help with the spelling as she went along. She wrote, "I love Jesus. I am sad because Jesus died on the cross. But Jesus rose from the dead on Easter and went to heaven."

On Easter Sunday when she came home from church she said, "I'm happy today!

Jesus rose from the dead. That's what Easter is about, you know. It's not just about Easter eggs and bunnies!"

This is the Orthodox Holy week. Here in Tirana I have seen a few small signs of this, but overall this is one of the least religious countries I have been in, no doubt partially a legacy of the strident atheism that was imposed on the population for the almost 50 years of Albania's harsh form of communism. I had hoped to attend an Orthodox service somewhere, but it did not work out this time, and I moved on to Romania over the weekend.

Romania, April 20, 1998, Orthodox Easter Monday

The first greeting I heard today as we arrived in the village of Baloga was *"CRISTOS A INVIAT !!*—Christ is risen!" We continued to get this greeting the rest of the day in this thoroughly Orthodox village. I learn the response—*A DE VERDAT!* He has Indeed!

What hospitality! They must have invented the word here. We visited 17 farm families. The pattern is the same in all of them: first friendly introductions, next we are brought to the barns to see their small herd of milk cows and then invited into their homes. They were very proud of the nice looking and good producing Romanian Simmental cows they received from Heifer, most of them with first calves. In most families, the woman takes care of the cows, but both men and women were proud of what they had to show us.

Each family invited us in for some homemade plum brandy, cakes, cheese, bread, cold meats and more. We had to refuse some of the invitations but ended up with a full lunch in the home of the association's president, Ovidio. The warmth from the wood-burning stove in the kitchen was more than equaled by the warmth of the people inside each home.

Ovidio made many references to Anna Zavada, Heifer's first Director of Programs for Eastern and Central Europe, who died recently of cancer. I have the privilege of following her footsteps and serving in this role on an interim basis. Anna's memory is cherished here because of the good this dairy-cow project has brought to Baloga. I think of Anna today and remember her inner and outer beauty and

171

how hard her dying was for her family and friends at Heifer. I remember her funeral at the Catholic Church in Little Rock, the celebration of her life and the words of hope spoken by the priest. It is appropriate to ponder these things during this Easter season. The glow and joy of Easter stays with these people for many days after Resurrection Sunday, and that spirit was contagious; I caught it too.

I remembered Romania as poorer and more run down, but now, after two visits to Albania, it looks wonderful. In fact, the road we were on today was in good shape and much improved since 1994 when I was here before. I am greatly enjoying this Easter day in Romania, despite the cold and rainy weather all day long!

Vadu Izei village—Northern Romania, April 21, 1998

The trip to the northernmost part of Transylvania was fantastic, especially scenic as we traversed the Maru Murish mountain range and descended down into the valley to this village very close to the Ukrainian border. I kept thinking that this is what the countryside and villages in Western Europe must have looked like 75 years ago. A colorful and well-composed picture was painted before my eyes: old wooden or brick houses clumped together in the village, surrounded by small farms, a variety of livestock, diminutive fields with tall haystacks on poles and families all out working the land with horses. The people here are trying to keep their proud identity and culture. They are poor by modern European standards, though hardly by a standard of traditional community values and life. With Romania's movement towards joining the European Economic Community, these farm families are going to need lots of help to raise their productivity in order to stay on the land. Modernization may well overwhelm them and accelerate a migration to the cities as has already happened in all industrialized and urbanized countries of Europe. That is the reason we are here, to help them stay on the land and prosper.

Ovidio Spinu (Heifer country representative in Romania) and I were staying in the home of Ion and Elena Borean and their two sons Alexander and Lorenzio. Besides farming a bit and offering hospitality in their home, Ion (John) is an artist who specializes in painting icons on glass. He is a kind and gentle person who

172

takes pleasure in showing and describing the icons he has created. I bought several from him. Then we gathered in their kitchen for pleasant and quiet conversation around the supper table. Soon I was tired and content to go upstairs to a cold bedroom. I nestled into the bed covered with a comforter in this quiet country cottage. It took me some time to fall asleep as I reveled in the mellow goodness of this place and this day.

Next morning: I awoke very early; yet I felt rested and at peace. It was so quiet here, though a neighbor's rooster did start to crow about 5:00 a.m. In my mind I heard the echo of the newly learned Romanian phrases, *"Cristos a inviat!"* and *"a de verdat."*

I read a bit from the Gospel of John about how we are connected to all people, going to the Father with Jesus and others. This house of John's, where I am staying, feels like a holy place where God is pleased to abide. This family knows who and where they are in relation to each other and to God. I wish I could stay here longer.

Cluj Napoca, Romania, April 24, 1998

On the return trip to the capitol of Transylvania, we had a flat tire and ended up in a communist-era spa for the night. It was very cold, and there was no heat in the room. It was dark when we arrived, so I did not see our surroundings then. In the morning, we awoke to see a glorious view of sun-drenched, snow-covered peaks, cold but clear and serene. It turns out this is actually a ski resort. As I gazed up, Psalm 121 came to mind again on this mountain as it has so many times before when beholding mountains, *I will lift my eyes unto the hills. From where does my help come?* I thanked the Lord for these few moments to absorb this corner of creation and splendor. What is it about rural life that I treasure so much? Well, Jesus did too . . . he generally avoided the cities and walked around the countryside. I think he would come here if he came back to earth today!

Now I had a few minutes of quiet in the kitchen of the Spinu's apartment. The sun was shining outside, a true spring day, about the first since I arrived in Europe.

Visions of Transylvania are fresh in my mind, but I fear I will soon forget the names of people and places as I tend to do from one trip to the next. For sure,

I will return here with Judy, maybe next year. I am privileged to be able to travel like this. Tourists normally don't have the opportunity to stay in a village home or monastery or take in the slower pace of life. I must admit, however, that our pace on this trip to the north was not as unhurried as I would have liked.

The cattle projects are working well. In fact, I think these efforts are accomplishing exactly what Heifer espouses to do, values-based development. Good livestock projects, group development, leadership, participation and spiritual and social values often exceed what we accomplish in the U.S.

I was literally in a post-Easter time during this trip, being reminded of it by the greetings and graciousness of the villagers we visited. But in the bigger and historical sense, I am always a post-Easter Christian, for what sense does my faith make without the resurrection? I have read some of the works on the historical Jesus, and much of what is written in the Gospels tells the stories of when Jesus walked on the earth before Easter. It is not so hard to believe that he was a great spiritual leader, a teacher of wisdom and a prophet, as well as a great preacher and doer of good for people. What takes the leap of faith is to know the post-Easter Jesus.

Reflection

At the end of his book on the historical Jesus, theologian Marcus Borg concludes with these words as he explains the meaning of the word believe.

> Believe did not originally mean believing in a set of doctrines or teachings; in both Greek and Latin its roots mean, "to give one's heart to." The "heart" is the self at its deepest level. Believing, therefore, does not consist of giving one's mental assent to something, but involves a much deeper level of one's self. Believing in Jesus does not mean believing doctrines about him. Rather, it means to give one's heart, one's self at the deepest level, to the post-Easter Jesus who is the living Lord, the side of God turned toward us, the face of God, the Lord who is also the Spirit (*Meeting Jesus Again for the First Time*, p. 137).

Meditation

*For if we have been united with him in a death like his, we will
certainly be united with him in a resurrection like his.*

Romans 6:5

- ☞ Elaborate for yourself specific ways in which the Easter message impacts your daily life long after Easter Sunday.

- ☞ The events of Holy Week are quite dramatic—the garden, the Last Supper, the crucifixion, the resurrection. Which of these events are the most emotionally charged for you?

- ☞ Jesus talked about the end of time. Imagine that the end of your life is tomorrow. Prioritize a list of what you would do today.

Faithful Servants

Well done, good and trustworthy slave; you have been trustworthy in a few things. I will put you in charge of many things.

Matthew 25:21

Warsaw, Poland, May 26, 1998

This is a trip to Poland and later to Ukraine where Heifer International is investigating the potential of starting a new program. I think I am prepared for this trip to Poland, but Ukraine might present some surprises. It stimulates my senses and imagination to be in former communist countries where there is so much cultural and political history and such tragic sagas of struggle over the last 60-plus years.

As I awoke in my hotel room I was pleasantly surprised to hear the singing of a superb male choir. I went out into the hall of my hotel and found that it was an Orthodox men's choir from Greece! I lay in bed listening to the deep, harmonious and pulsating sounds echoing throughout the hotel. I enjoyed the melodic lines of the chant and allowed myself to listen with my heart. I found the beautiful and mysterious sound of it soothing and soon I was totally relaxed and nodded off.

May 30, 1998

We drove south through the Polish countryside on our way to the village of Zegocina, passing through the city of Bochnia. We have a project here, so we stopped for a brief visit. Here we met with Father Antonio, the local priest and one of the project leaders. He had just attended a ceremony commemorating the 800th anniversary of the founding of this town! Christianity came before the town in 966—so they have already celebrated the 1,000-year anniversary.

Meeting Fr. Antonio gave me cause for reflection and thanksgiving for the faithful service of this good man. A priest here has high status in the community, not only in the church. Fortunately, this priest is interested in the economic welfare of his people as well as the spiritual.

We got to Zegocina in the afternoon with enough time to visit farm families and meet with leaders of the project. I was pleased to see that much attention was given to the role and importance of women and children; and I was lifted up and encouraged by what I saw and heard. As we visited the family farms, the women and men both talked animatedly and proudly of their small farms and what they produced, especially the fine looking dairy cows they received from the project.

In Zegocina, we are told that when the news of Anna Zewada's death came in February, they held a mass in her honor in the village church. Anna, whose native country was Poland, was Heifer's Central and Eastern Europe director. After she died of cancer, I was asked to fill her shoes temporarily, a tall order, indeed. My heart warms, and my eyes get misty when I hear how these rural people loved and honored Anna.

Zegocina, Pentecost Sunday, May 31, 1998

I awoke several times during the night, read a bit and then fell back to sleep. I finally arose at 6:00 to stretch and pray. The fresh scent of hay came into the room through the open windows; birds sang; a rooster crowed; and a dove cooed. The earth was alive as the sun came over the mountain and warmed me. The yard of the house across the alley has a small greenhouse, a couple of large sheds, trees, cats and a hen with chicks. An elderly lady walked about the barnyard attending to morning chores. Soon more colorful chickens appeared, including a rooster. Large and small birds flew back and forth, a beautiful morning in the foothills of the Carpathian Mountains in the south of Poland! Though I enjoyed this setting immensely, I was away from home and have been separated from Judy for some days already. It would be nice to be with her this morning, either here or there! When we went to the church at 9:00 o'clock there was an overflow crowd, but we pushed our way in and stood in the back.

Southern Poland, June 2, 1998

We visited Heifer's largest and oldest project in this country. The project has delivered good quality dairy cows to several hundred small-holder farmers, and these families took great pride in their accomplishments as they showed us around.

After numerous farm visits, we ended up sitting around the kitchen table in the house of Mr. and Mrs. Bruzda. In this congenial atmosphere, Mr. Bruzda told a story. He said that he suffered a stroke last year and nearly died. He now feels much better, and his wife affirms that he, indeed, does look better, though he walks with a cane and suffers some paralysis. His story sounded like a near death experience.

His wife relates that after he had the stroke and was in the hospital, the family had accepted the worst. They were quite sure he was going to die. But, Mr. Bruzda said, "In the hospital I had a vision. I was in a room that was all blue. The room was intensely lit, and on the wall I saw something written. It said "Your years of faithful service with the Heifer project counts for something for you." He interpreted this to mean that it counted for good with God, and he was allowed to come back to his family again. Bruzda was very serious and thoughtful as he related this story to us, and we listened with intense interest. Smiling, we affirmed that his interpretation was probably true! As we drove away we reflected on this experience, wondering about what we had just seen and heard, pondering all these things, as it were. It would seem that the vision of this project has penetrated to the very core of these people.

Lublin, Poland, June 12, 1998

On the highway that leads to Lublin, we saw a sign for Majdenek. Professor Jasorowrski thought it would be interesting for us to stop and see this site, a Nazi concentration camp. It was very quiet as we entered and started our walking tour. No staff was visible, no visitor's center, though written information was available in several languages.

Constructed in 1941, Majdenek was liberated on August 30, 1945. The grim statistics are these: 300,000 people were sent here by the Nazis of whom 235,000 were exterminated in gas chambers or executed by firing squads. Over 60 percent were Jews. One day the killing was at a fever pitch: on November 3, 1943, 18,400 Jews were shot to death. What was then a site of the worst kind of human degradation, today, 55 years later, is quiet, set in the tranquility of a green hilltop surrounded by grassy fields.

Of course we have heard such stories many times in documentaries, novels, and movies: the massive numbers arriving, scared and bewildered, sent to "baths" which were instead gas chambers, the concrete slabs where corpses were cut open in search of valuables, mostly gold from teeth. Some were forced to work at the unspeakably horrific job of removing the bodies of those who were shot.

In silence we walked through the barracks, the crematorium, and the gas chamber. We tried to imagine how it looked and felt when 800 people were stuffed into these barracks—the three-tiered bunks, the diet of less than 1,000 calories for people forced to do hard labor, typhus and other diseases weakening and decimating their bodies.

We moved too quickly through it all as a gentle rain began, reading information on small signs and looking at artifacts. My stomach tensed and revolted, yet my mind played with the facts presented as if another history lesson. We stood right there on the very spot where such evil was carried out. We paused for a while in front of the large pile of ashes, the only remains of thousands. We repeated to each other the words that have been said by countless other visitors before us, "How could this have happened?"

Yet there is hope and faith even here. One exhibit shows holy writ: prayers in thin booklets, the Torah, and Bibles found in the belongings. Are these signs that some or many called upon God in their despair. When stripped of all rudiments of their humanity, they reached deep inside and looked for God in a place the killers could not reach and maybe even found peace at the last. Were some of those who wrought this evil brought to repentance? We can only wonder. Poland leaves me with things to ponder.

And so I ponder about and remember one of my spiritual heroes. His name was Gabor Sztehlo, a pastor of the Lutheran Church of Hungary. His sojourn through life from his birth in Hungary to the mountaintop in the Swiss Alps where he died, affected many people, in fact, saved many people during those dark days of World War II when the Nazis cast their dreadful shadow over most of Europe. He wrote part of his story in a book called *In the Hands of God*.

Had he been reading his Bible when he died or perhaps some of the letters the postman had delivered, letters from some of the children he had saved from the Nazis? The neighbors found him sitting on the bench by the village church he was serving in Switzerland during the last years of his ministry. When I heard about it, I thought, "What a good way to go, alone with the Word of God, a view of a brilliant glacier towering above!" I wondered, "were his last thoughts about the majesty of creation, the grandeur of the mountain peaks, the peacefulness of the day, or was he reflecting on those days long ago in the valleys of his life?"

I encountered him only briefly in the summer of 1968 when he was very helpful in arranging a chalet for us to stay during a hiking holiday in the Alps. My best friend, Marlyn, had married Gabor's daughter, Ildiko, and they were living in England in 1968, the year Judy and I traveled through Europe on the way home from Vietnam. We stopped to visit Marlyn and Ildi and rest a bit after our two years of service in that war zone. Our families took a trip together to Switzerland.

Now I think back, and I wish I had taken more time to talk with him to learn about his life and what he could tell me about suffering and evil, about grace and faithfulness.

In 1943 the Nazis invaded and occupied Budapest. The bishop told this young pastor—"Pastor Sztehlo, you need to do something to help the persecuted and those threatened with death." This meant the Jews of Budapest, especially the children. Sometimes an answer to prayer can be horrifying, "O Lord, do something to save the children!" "OK," God said, "You do it in my name."

Sztehlo went to work immediately and recruited dozens of volunteers, found safe houses, organized children's havens under the banner of the Swiss Red Cross and negotiated with the Nazis. It was humbling, exhausting, terrifying and exhilarating. Later he wrote, "In the end all I could do was put it in the hands of God." He didn't say, "I don't have any experience for this kind of thing so let somebody else do it." He didn't give the excuse that he was trained to be a pastor and didn't want to get involved in risky political work.

The result was that over 900 Jewish children and 635 adults were saved! Yes, literally saved—It's as good a story as Shindler's List, but it has never been made into a movie.

That meeting in 1968 was the first and only time I ever saw him. I remember his handsome, kind and rugged face, his smile and the thick shock of wavy gray hair. He didn't impose on our time up on the mountain that week. He let us have our holiday, enjoying the beauty and time to unwind, even though his grandchildren were with us on our hikes and picnics in the beauty of the Alps. Why didn't he join us during our time up there? Maybe it was his heart. He had already had a heart attack, but he did have a very big heart!

For Gabor Sztehlo his work of rescue was a test of faith. In his memoir he wrote, "Christianity is not the world of dogmas, but of love—of a living, lively and active love."

Years later I visited the Holocaust Museum in Washington D.C. I had visited several concentration camps in Poland before this, and this museum offers a realistic depiction of those horrific places. At the end of the museum tour, there is a display called the Rescuers' Wall. There you see the names of gentiles, non-Jewish people from many countries, who risked their lives to defend and save Jews during the holocaust.

I looked at the short list of names from Hungary, and with a chill running down my spine and a catch in my breath, I saw his name, Gabor Sztehlo. I stood transfixed for a few moments, remembering, pondering and thankful. I was thankful for having encountered this good man ever so briefly those many years ago, a small encounter on my own walk through life. He was a faithful servant of God and had done well.

Reflection

In a preface to the journal Gabor Sztehlo kept in 1944, he wrote:

> The year 1944 was especially significant for me, for this was the year when I realized that God guides me, defends and guards me in my deeds. In the last year of World War II, people would daily ask me questions like: Where is God now? Why does He let all this happen? If God really is love, why does He allow His chosen people to suffer so much? Is God really just? Where is He who loves justice? and Why is tyranny rampant and God just allows it? Later people stopped asking such questions.
>
> I cannot help wondering even today at how we still keep badgering our Lord with so many unnecessary questions in spite of all our knowledge and experiences. . . . Priests or not, we all have to start anew with the basics and never stop learning thereafter. We seem to find it so hard to understand that all of Creation is God's property. But He loves us; He acts for us; and by sacrificing His son, He gave to us the greatest sacrifice possible. When will we finally take in this sole and most important lesson—this good news? (*In the Hands of God*, p. 7).

Pastor Stezhlo was thinking about questions that plagued people in the midst of their worst experiences. He prayed with and for the people who were struggling so mightily with questions and experiences of war, suffering and sin.

Meditation

*Deal with your servant according to your steadfast love,
and teach me your statutes. I am your servant; give me understanding,
so that I may know your decrees.*

Psalm 119:124, 125

☞ Reflect for a moment on one person you have encountered who lived what you believe to be a faithful life. What were this person's qualities that impressed you? What were the lasting effects that this person had on you?

☞ The maturing of our faith occurs as we grow through struggles, doubts and challenges. Of the many struggles of faith you have had, reflect on one that was the most memorable for you and take note of what helped you to live through that challenge.

☞ Write your own epitaph. What words would you like to have etched on your cemetery headstone that will be remembered by friends and family?

Irritations

Paul referred to glorying in bad experiences, and the Gospel speaks of signs of the kingdom in the most ordinary happenings.

Joseph Schmidt

The Las Vegas airport, *February 20, 2007*

I just left my peaceful little Montana town. Two days ago I was skiing near our home where I paused frequently on runs down the mountain to take in the breathtaking beauty. When I stopped to rest for a moment to regain strength in my legs, I was mindful of the grandeur of creation. Nearly out of breath from exertion, but also from the exhilaration, the only sound I heard was that of my breath and my beating heart. Sometimes I could hear the breeze through the pine trees. Often when I am in settings like this, alone in the silence, I utter a word of thanks that I have this mountain practically to myself, and I am filled with gratitude.

Where I sit right now is not an oasis of quiet in the desert. It is a market place of noise and commotion. There is a hum of background music, not even the kind of music I like. Talk and shrill laughter is interrupted by the blaring announcement—"Standby passenger Kelly, please report to the podium." Then, . . . "Testing—one, two, three—Thank you for your patience." We now invite passengers in zones 1, 2, and 3 to board." What patience? I ask myself.

I am trying to read! But "This is the final and immediate call for . . ." loudly breaks into my consciousness. Behind me someone talks incessantly on a cell phone. This is the daily din and background noise for thousands, yes millions of people. I wonder if this is normal. Do human beings adapt to this? Maybe there is something about us humans that craves incessant sound. Or is there something

184

within us that craves silence? I suspect the truth is that humans flee from silence and fear it!

Again I try to focus on reading, but to no avail. The points being made in the devotional I am reading mix with the distractions. After several times rereading the same paragraph, I wonder, "What was Ezekiel talking about? Visions of four-faced beings, wheels in the sky . . . there must be a point here." But I give it up as it is too hard to grasp in this noisy atmosphere.

Now I have to get up and change seats in the waiting area. A woman seated immediately across from me talks loudly on her cell phone. It seems to be a totally one-sided conversation, her side. Irritated, I get up and move.

What am I to make of these irritations? Is there a lesson here?

I have Henri Nouwen's book *The Way of the Heart* with me as reading material for this trip. It is a book about solitude and silence. Henri promises to instruct me in solitude, silence and prayer, and I eagerly anticipate it. Lent starts tomorrow, and I hope there will be interludes of silence and peacefulness during this trip.

But now another announcement—"Flight 864 is ready for immediate boarding and departure." I get up, join the line and obediently descend into the belly of the beast.

———

You might be wondering what I was doing in the Las Vegas airport with Nouwen, journaling about irritations and, at the same time, showing the flaws in my own personality. I was on my way to El Salvador for Agros International. It is always a bit of a transition to prepare for a trip, leave home, travel and get into the next cultural context. One of the greatest challenges of the kind of work I undertook for four decades was to move from one culture to another in a short period of time. That is the nature of the world in which we now live. We can travel from the comforts of our opulence to poor communities in a few hours. But in reality, we are transitioning from extremes of human experience, from wealth to poverty, from safety to turmoil, and from overabundance to subsistence. This is a transition of generations, not of hours. This is shown in the next journal entries in a completely different context.

Maputu, Mozambique, January 17, 1998

I have returned to the backwaters of Africa. This is a tropical, underdeveloped, ex-colonial, failed Marxist, poor, dirty and rundown country, not unlike Nicaragua and Albania, where I have recently traveled. This is yet another new country for me, and I eventually find something I like in every country I visit. I have only vague notions and a broad outline of its history. It was a Portuguese colony. Portugal was perhaps the worst of the European colonizers, keeping people uneducated and oppressed for more than a century. Mozambique finally gained independence in 1973. After that the country fell into chaos and civil war for 20 years. An armed struggle developed along the lines of classic cold war alliances: the Marxist government of Somora Marchel fighting the guerillas supported by South Africa and perhaps the U.S. I get irritated with geopolitical conflicts and power struggles at the expense of the poor.

Over the last four or five years a degree of peace and stability has returned. The international community has moved in with the usual structural adjustments of the IMF (International Monetary Fund) and the U.S. and South Africa have interest in seeing stability and prosperity here. This is related to the reason for my being here. Heifer Project has a large U.S. government grant for a goat project which we have been running for several years. My first impression is that this place, indeed, does fit our criteria for genuine need.

Mozambique, Sunday, January 18, 1998

I enjoyed my early morning physical and spiritual exercises. This morning I arose before 5:00 a.m., slowly got going, stretched, dressed in exercise clothes and read a portion of Scripture from Romans about prayer as "too deep for words." Then I went out to walk, run and see. There were lots of broken sidewalks, potholes, garbage and litter to skip over and walk around. I went down to a boardwalk overlooking the sea, and here I saw a few upscale apartment buildings, the occupants walking their poodles accompanied by private guards. Yet, even here there is a feel of scarcity, not opulence. Then I ran and walked about a mile down the beach and found a place to sit in the quiet of the morning. I have been reading about the prayer of presence in Marjorie Thompson's book. I practiced it. "Breathe in peace—breathe out tension." It was wonderful to gaze out at the ocean as the sun came up, though it was not completely quiet even at this hour.

186

A pulsating drumbeat boomed in the distance, yet it actually did not disturb me. In fact it was rather soothing. I was trying to figure out if this was the last vestige of an all-night party or maybe an early Sunday morning Pentecostal Church service.

Walking back to the *penseo* (the Inn), I passed by two street children, boys about ten years old, sleeping on the sidewalk. One had a cloth bunched up under his head for a pillow, the other's head rested on the crook of his arm. They were clothed in dirty shorts and ragged shirts, no shoes, their bodies dusty and their scant garments caked with dirt and grime like a mechanics overall.

This scene caused a sense of affective dissonance within me; it was a shocking contrast to the peacefulness and calm of my earlier time of prayer and meditation. It was a miniscule example of the injustice in the world economic order. But then, again, they looked quite peaceful as they slept there on the concrete.

I was quickly shown the needs of the world and the grinding poverty of the vulnerable. I just walked into it. I thought how it is that in noticing, just keeping my eyes open, that I am made aware of the consequences of sin and the needs of the world in which I live. I was forced to empathize with the children's situation, not only to think about their condition and understand it. I paused and wondered about their daily existence and struggle for survival. I cannot imagine where they would find a sense of hope.

In the end, I did nothing more than pause and walk on, aware of my feelings, leaving these two little ones to sleep on in the morning sunshine. What could I do? What would you do? Or Jesus? I wondered. This scene that symbolized the sins of the world is not God pleasing.

I know that those of us who support and work in social and economic development programs do it because of the inhuman and unjust conditions in which so many live. But, I think to myself, I am not involved in an urban project with street children. Isn't it enough to just walk by, to say a short prayer of intercession, to make the sign of the cross? That was my gut reaction. But I felt deep down that it was not sufficient. I jotted down this quote, which I must have recently heard. I don't know where it comes from or who said it. "That is why each of us does what we do each day. We do it to remember *daiyehnu*—there is enough to share!"

Quilimane, Mozambique, January 20, 1998

We flew 100 kilometers north to this city on the coast. Here Heifer International has a small office out of which the project is administered. It is very hot and sticky here. The rainy season is in full swing so everything is muddy and wet. Joel, our in-country representative, is an old Africa hand. He has us staying in a large and dilapidated plantation house he rented for us outside of town. It is called *Chaumbo Dumbe,* but I don't know what that means. To reach it we traveled over an atrocious road. The house has no electricity and no water, and Joel said, "You can't trust the workers." He thinks they have stolen from him. It is dark and damp, but other than that it is a really elegant place to stay! I would not last long in these conditions, yet Joel is sort of indifferent to his surroundings and seems to have simple needs. I slept all right, though I awoke feeling groggy and sticky. I am never totally comfortable sleeping in the hot tropics.

We have a large goat distribution program here. It is not the best-managed program, but then this is a very difficult place to manage anything. Thousands of goats have been purchased in the neighboring country of Zimbabwe, but there are poor records to show how many have been distributed to how many people. Yet things are improving, and the reason we are here is to help get the record keeping and management situation in better shape.

I see much hunger here. It is obvious on the faces and bodies of the children who beg from us in each place we eat. There are signs of *kwashiorkor* (childhood malnutrition). Discolored and thinning hair and distended bellies are obvious on their small frames. I gave some leftover beans to a boy who quickly gobbled them down.

January 21

Out in the countryside we visited a group that has received goats and a receiving center where goats are held when they come into the country before distribution to community groups. It is terribly hot! I sweat and sweat all day long. I am surprised to see that the countryside is quite sparsely populated, since it looks to me like there is potential for agriculture here. There is lots of bush, second-growth trees, bad roads and very poor people. The only vehicles we see belong to development NGOs like ours or to government officials.

188

Joel speaks in a loud and squeaky voice. He squints and says things that he alone sees humor in and then laughs at his joke or the irony of what he is saying. I get irritated with him, but realize I need to pull back and not be too forceful or defensive. No need to get stressed. Things take time to work out.

In John 14, Jesus is quoted as saying, *Do not let your hearts be troubled. Believe in God, believe also in me.* I am noticing lots of things Jesus said about prayer, and I realize that we are just to ask in His name. My prayer for now is for inner peace and the wisdom to show that peace to others. Usually I am perceived as a pretty levelheaded person, one who figures things out and offers good recommendations for improving programs. There is much that is wrong with this program, but none of it is easy to correct, I think. I am not always so calm and levelheaded these days.

These people live in horrible conditions after the long years of war and deprivation. With few resources and little education, the odds are stacked against them. Actually, I wouldn't want to be in Joel's shoes. He is trying his best to administer a program here. It is hard to find people to take on assignments in conditions like these.

January 23, 1998

It is our wedding anniversary today, another one separated from Judy. She sent me an email telling me she is lonely and that she bought some flowering plants to put on the table to remember our 33rd anniversary. How many times have we been apart on this special day? The demands of my work over the years have often meant travel at this time of the year. I remember a time some years ago on a lonely evening in an East African country, I think Zimbabwe. I wrote in my journal that I thought I should stop all this travel and separation from Judy. Now here I am, a dozen years later, in the same situation. My work and career in international development has been an immense privilege and satisfaction. But I cannot deny that there are days like this when I wish I were at home and not in these displeasing surroundings. I pray for Judy this morning that she is at peace and enjoying the day. She has invited some girlfriends down to the farm to watch the Super Bowl.

I took an early morning walk again to center myself and enjoy the peaceful presence of God as I sat and gazed at the skyline on the sea's horizon. I did pretty well in not allowing the distractions and irritations to intrude—this time. But, I wonder, what am I to do with my inclination to impatience and irritation? How do I incorporate these into my spiritual life?

Reflection

Joseph Schmidt offers these thoughts:

> For many of us, in our efforts to develop a relationship with God, humanness seems to be part of the problem. We wish that we did not have human difficulties. We wish that we did not have to struggle with this or that human predicament. We want to rise above our humanness. We take the soaring impulses of our spirit to mean that our humanness, with all its finiteness, stupidity, and foolishness, is too limited and too ungodly to be of value. There is often a curious and subtle wish to be angelic.

> Sometimes we deny our humanness; sometimes we reject our humanness; mostly we are quietly afraid of it—of the uncontrollability of its demands, of its limitations and inevitable slide to death. We are simply embarrassed about our humanness and wish that it would go away. We wish that our human concerns were over so that we could pray . . . but . . . the mystery of the incarnation means that our human concerns are concerns of God and that our task is to accept and appreciate human life as human life and not to reject it as lesser angelic life. Jesus came that we would have this human life, with abundance, not with embarrassment or fear or reluctance (*Praying Our Experiences,* pp. 56, 57).

Meditation

*But I say to you that if you are angry with a brother or sister,
you will be liable to judgment. . . . So when you are offering a gift at
the altar, if you remember that your brother or sister has something
against you, leave your gift before the altar and go; first be reconciled to
your brother or sister, and then come and offer your gift.*

Matthew 5: 22, 23

☞ What situations and relationships test your patience and irritate you?

☞ What insight have you learned about yourself from your patterns of impatience?

☞ How do feelings of impatience, irritation, anger and self-pity affect your daily life?

☞ How do you deal with distractions and irritations in your work life? In your prayer life? In your relationships?

Doubt in Albania

For everything there is a season, and a time for every matter under heaven: a time to break down and a time to build up.

Ecclesiastes 3:1, 3b

Albania, October 5, 1997

On my way to Albania, I read in a devotional message that God is with us. These words give me comfort when I face unknown situations and places, and this certainly qualifies as one of those. My route took me to Vienna and then to Tirana, the capitol of Albania. In all my years of school and study, I never learned a thing about this country, so I am now reading about it. More than most countries I have visited, this is almost a complete blank.

First impressions! It is sunny and warm, and the people in the organization I am going to work with are friendly. Daut, the Heifer International representative in Albania, met me and we went to his tiny apartment, where I met his daughter, Ina, and wife, Lela. We climbed the broken and dingy stairway to their apartment on the fifth floor. It is crowded, drab and dark, without a balcony to the outside. I tried not to show it, but I was taken aback by these dreary and spartan accommodations. It is the kind of housing found in former communist countries, large blocks of un-creatively designed apartment complexes—totally drab. During the communist regime, Daut was a professional in the government's animal husbandry department, a position of some importance. All families were provided with housing, but there is an obvious lack of quality in the living spaces of these buildings.

These are pleasant people. I like them immediately, and we exchange stories of our families, who we are and where we have been. After the customary hospitality

192

of drinking a toast with raki, the strong, clear alcohol drink everywhere present in Albania, we left for the office.

Later Daut received a call from his daughter telling him that Lela's father had just died. Daut was shaken by this unexpected news and changed his plan to accompany me on a field trip the next day. He said that I will still go, but now with someone else. I said a few words of condolence as Daut rushed off to be with his wife. I couldn't help but wonder how these family members, who are nominally Muslim, in a country that has been officially atheist for decades, deal with the death of loved ones.

In the late afternoon I strolled out onto the streets where I saw a large gathering of people, a political rally of some sort. A sign was held by one of the demonstrators that read, "Stop the communist killers!" in English and Albanian. I took pictures, but no one noticed; there is not even an echo of the former repression here. The streets are dirty, dusty and garbage-strewn, but many people were walking around, sitting in cafes drinking coffee and enjoying each other's company. They were engaged in animated conversations in smoke-filled rooms, talking enthusiastically, about what—I don't have a clue. Most of my career, I have been able to communicate with the people in countries where I travel and work, either in Spanish, English, or my minimal Portuguese, but in Eastern Europe, without an interpreter, I am lost. Few speak English here. A sign on the bathroom wall of my hotel reads:

"Clients pleased to not throw towels or cleaned shoes down."

What does that mean? I am puzzled, but will try to pay strict attention to this rule while staying at this hotel.

I have noticed in other countries, too, where the populace lives in cramped quarters, people come out onto the streets and walk around, especially in the late afternoon, congregating in the plazas and town squares. I try to empathize with what life must have been like in Albania for decades under communism. It is always a stretch to put myself in the shoes of others (cleaned or not!) with such different experiences.

For decades this was one of the most isolated, repressive, paranoid, atheistic and dreary countries in the communist world. Albania split off from Tito's Yugoslavia, from the Soviets and even from Mao. Those countries were all too revisionist! I have been in a number of countries where people lived under dictatorship, but from what I have read, Albania's dictator, Hoxha, and his cronies did much evil here. The question crept into my mind, "What happens to dictators when they die?" I remember bull sessions back in college that posed the question, "Could Hitler have been redeemed?" Whatever else can be said, it is true that the Albanian people were held under calamitous repression and that Albania was the poorest country in Europe throughout the cold war and into the post-communist era, as well.

⸺◈⸺

God holds creation together in spite of human attempts to tear it apart. In Colossians 1:17, we read, *He himself is before all things, and in him all things hold together.* This is a country that is having difficulty holding things together.

After the Albanian people overthrew their taskmasters in 1991, the reaction of the population was a destructive and hysterical release of emotion and anger. We went to the Agricultural University and saw some of the results of this. Rioting crowds had sacked all the buildings, burned the library and all its books, destroyed desks and labs, cut down vineyards and trees and busted up greenhouses and classrooms. Not only here, but around the country, the violence left people dead in the streets. And now Albanians try to get out of their country like rats fleeing a sinking ship. Tens of thousands are going to Italy. The U.S. government and many NGOs are here to help create a democratic and prosperous country; that will be a long and slow process.

October 8, 1997

This was a good day in the village of Kallmet where Heifer's first project in Albania, a village group working with swine, is underway. Daut accompanied me. The common wisdom here is that "working together" in Albania is difficult, too much distrust from years of oppression and forced participation. So I am here to assess "group formation" and make recommendations about how to increase participation and build trust. Wow! There has been a "time to tear apart, and (we

194

hope) a time to mend" here in Albania. I am enough of a realist to know that someone coming in from the outside for a few weeks is not going to make a big difference. But I try.

Life in the village seems more peaceful and of higher quality than life in the city. But that is often my feeling, maybe my bias, as I compare rural and urban life wherever I travel and work. Certainly the houses are bigger and more livable than Daut's flat back in Tirana. This village is 100 percent Catholic, and the people are restoring their church, which had gone into almost complete disrepair. It was used as a warehouse during the Hoxha regime. There is a revival of sorts happening in Albania, almost a competition of building churches and mosques.

There is much to rebuild here. Factories were abandoned, churches destroyed, public buildings in disrepair, all this while 700,000 bunkers were built in preparation for the attacks that were expected to come from the West. It is said that each bunker consumed as much concrete as it would have taken to build an apartment for one family. I wonder about our small efforts to re-establish trust and hope for the future given the legacy left by such a suspicious system. We shall see more of this effort in the coming days. My hope is to see people rebuilding their lives, too, not only the buildings. But I have my doubts.

A visit to Shengergj, October 10, 1997

This is a village high in the rocky and forest-covered mountains to the east of Tirana. To get here we traveled through misty and cloud-shrouded valleys where families are farming and tending livestock on small plots of land. The term "summer pastures" took on meaning for me as we climbed up to visit an old couple in their shack on the side of the mountain, tending their goats and sheep during the summer and fall. They welcomed us into the comfort of a room heated by a potbellied stove, a much-appreciated escape from the cold and wet weather outside. Here the cliché "going back a century in time" more or less applies, though that long ago there would not have been a road to bring foreign and city visitors in four-wheel drive vehicles. My heart was warmed, as was my body, while we sat and chatted for some minutes with this elderly couple.

This is a Muslim village, though apparently few are strict practitioners of their religion here or in Albania in general. Daut says he is a Muslim but certainly not a practicing one. I worry about his drinking; though this seems merged with the "cultural appropriateness" of Albanian hospitality, as we are obliged to toast with and drink raki at every stop.

October 15, 1997

When I went back to Trashon, the problem village, we had a very lively meeting with about 25 farmers, including eight women. Though they did not come to a decision, many opinions and ideas were aired, and I detected some movement toward trust and reconciliation. Daut said that he was a Muslim and others there were Christians, but that we have the same God. "It is just that we have different names to call God," he said. In my heart, I can grasp truth in that view; though I am not fully in accord with the theology of it. Nevertheless, my prayer is that the God of peace and love will be present through the Spirit in this troubled land, and in my heart I believe that to be the Spirit of Jesus. I accept that many of these Muslims are at least as devout as I am, probably more so. After all, we both share the Abrahamic faith tradition.

Normally I am not one to complain and criticize a country I am visiting, but as I prepared to leave, I made a list of likes and dislikes. Many of them, unfortunately for me, are on the downside. At this point in history, not much is working in this country—infrastructure is in bad shape; no jobs are being created; old structures being torn apart and not being replaced by something that works. But on the positive side, there is an overall friendliness and hospitality toward foreigners. In the villages the people are trying to get ahead. I spent many hours in village meetings and farm visits being fed, toasted and made to feel welcome.

When I left Albania, I knew it was likely I would never return.

Reflection

Daut was an especially congenial and amiable person, though prone to unhealthy lifestyle habits. I remember one morning when we started out early to visit a village. About 9:00 o'clock we stopped at a small café, and he said, "Jerry, would you like to stop for a cognac? I think you need a cognac!" He was a heavy smoker, a good-natured drinker of raki, and a bit overweight. He did little in the line of exercise. He had already suffered several heart attacks at that time, and we encouraged him to go to Italy for treatment, which his doctor recommended and his family urged him to do.

When I heard of his death from heart disease several years later, I was not surprised, but the news brought back memories of a good man who had lived most of his life in hard times. I believe he could answer his God that he had lived a useful life on earth. I don't think of Albania often, but when I do, I think of Daut and his assertion that we "all have the same God," and I wonder about that. Encountering diverse cultural and faith traditions will do that to you; it makes you wonder—and sometimes doubt.

Meditation

Jesus said, "Have faith in God . . . and if you do not doubt in your heart, but believe that what you say will come to pass, it will be done for you.

Mark 11:22, 23

☞ Have you ever experienced culture shock—a time when the geography, the people or the language were so totally new to you that you felt disorientated? If so, describe your feelings and emotions. At that moment how did you handle your reactions?

☞ How do harsh or unfamiliar settings affect your spiritual journey and prayer life?

☞ What do you think about the notion that there is One God of all, who is called by different names in different faith traditions? Is this idea compatible with your understanding of Christian faith?

197

Celebration

Then the father said to him, "Son, you are always with me,
and all that is mine is yours. But we had to celebrate and rejoice,
because this brother of yours was dead and has come to life,
he was lost and has been found."

Luke 15:31, 32

Pushkin, near St Petersburg, Russia, June 10, 2003

I am here to lead a workshop with Heifer International staff on how to address
the needs of children and youth at risk, not just here in Russia but all around the
world. About 40 participants have come from all the continents where Heifer
works. It is good to be with friends and colleagues from many countries who
belong to this Heifer family. Yesterday our event opened with much fanfare and
ceremony, including a marching band with bugles, drums and wind instruments
and raising the "Heifer flag," an opening ceremony the likes of which I have never
experienced in dozens of workshops and conferences I have been part of over the
years with Heifer. It was an extraordinary kick-off for our conference and started
us out in high spirits, even though I felt a bit embarrassed for all the attention.

Last night was the opening banquet with classical music performed by a string
quartet joined for some pieces by trumpet, a world-class pianist and a soprano
opera singer. Also, a lovely and graceful female dancer performed for us. My
emotional and spiritual senses were filled to the brim. I was happy to be here.
At the same time I felt a touch of dissonance as I thought of the cost and
elaborateness of this event in comparison to the humble beginnings of Heifer and
its founder, Dan West. He was a totally frugal man from humble American rural
roots. While I do not wish to dampen the spirit of celebration and merriment, I

198

think it is right to keep a perspective on our spiritual roots and purposes, that of service to the poor, who cannot be at any banquet table today. So I try to keep equilibrium and focus on the hoped-for outcomes of this conference, how to serve the youth and children of the world better through our efforts.

Pushkin, June 12, 2003

Early this morning the Spirit prompted me to read about joy. I have been reading Henri Nouwen's book *The Return of the Prodigal Son: A Story of Homecoming*. Now that I am so near I am determined to go to the Hermitage Museum in St. Petersburg to see the famous Rembrandt painting on which this book is based.

Will what Henri writes help me with my dilemma about the balancing of costs of celebration and the needs of others? He says,

> I realize that I am not used to the image of God throwing a party. Among the ways Jesus describes the Kingdom of God is the feast . . . especially the wedding feast. In the story of the Prodigal son, the father "kills the fatted calf" and throws a party—much to the chagrin of the older brother.

These thoughts give me cause to reflect on my sour attitude when I felt critical of my colleagues and hosts about all the feasting and partying at our event here in Russia. I realize that they gave this party to honor (and impress) us, the guests. So I try to be happy and see joy in all things, even as we are discussing the serious themes of this conference. Again from Henri, "People who have come to know the joy of God do not deny the darkness, but they choose not to live in it."

St. Petersburg, June 15, 2003

My last day in St. Petersburg: The conference went well, and I am pleased that concrete plans were made for follow-up. Now the group is dispersing to far-flung points of the globe, but about half of us are still here to take the midnight excursion of the canals of St Petersburg and the Neva River . . . the full treatment of the white nights. What a fantastic city Peter the Great built. It is overwhelming to consider the wealth it took, the sacrifice of millions, the ingenuity and the importance of impressing the rest of the world with their accomplishments.

Today, Trinity Sunday, I will try to get to the Hermitage to see Rembrandt's *Prodigal Son*. I have been reflecting on this parable and Henri's interpretations of it all week. Our Russian colleagues do not encourage this outing, saying it will be a huge crowd and too much of a hassle. I want to go anyway, especially to see the Rembrandt, and I pray that the Spirit will open my eyes to see it outwardly and inwardly and to understand, appreciate and know in some deeper way this great teaching of Jesus.

St. Petersburg, June 16, 2003

I was able to go to the Hermitage, and though it was a hasty visit, it was a thrill I shall always remember. The place was crowded with thousands of tourists. I separated from the small group I was with and made my way to the room with the Rembrandt painting. I stood alone before this great piece of art while literally hundreds of tourists passed by individually or in tour groups. French-, Russian-, Japanese-, German- and English-speaking guided groups passed by. Each of them spent only a few minutes to take it in and then rushed on to the next must-see piece of art.

I overheard the English-speaking guide explaining, "Now, this is a picture by the famous Dutch artist Rembrandt of a story from the Bible. This one is called the Prodigal Son and is about a young man who . . ." She went on to paraphrase the story. It was a moment of delight for me as I realized that this was really the Gospel text being read and interpreted to these people on this Sunday morning, almost certainly the only Scripture they would hear today. How great is that? A five-hundred-year-old piece of art is sharing the truth of this ancient text like a homily in a worship service with these secular, modern people of Europe.

Reflection

Nouwen observed the blessing of the father's hands, and I see it as he described:

> The left one is a strong, masculine hand with a firm grasp on his son's shoulder, receiving his son back home and holding him close.

200

The right hand is soft and lies gently on the shoulder of the son, offering consolation and comfort . . . a mother's hand. The figure of the father, of course, shows how God accepts, forgives and is generous. He orders everyone to be merry and have a party. Great joy because the one whom he loves so much and whom he thought was lost has come home.

Jesus, of course, meant to teach us about God's love flowing out generously for those who come to God, for those who may have strayed away and longed for reconciliation. It is God the Father's big and joyful party to receive and embrace us. I felt that message in the reading of Nouwen's book, and I saw it again in viewing the Rembrandt portrayal.

Meditation

So he set off and went to his father. But while he was still far off,
his father saw him and was filled with compassion; he ran
and put his arms around him and kissed him.

Luke 15:20

⌇ Read and meditate on the entire parable of the Prodigal Son in Luke 15: 11-32. In what ways do you identify with a specific character in the Parable—the prodigal son, the father, the older son, or the mother?

⌇ What is your favorite day of celebration? Why?

⌇ Is there a special, even iconic, piece of art that you have been attracted to, that prompts you to ponder and to reflect on faith and spiritual life? What does this artifact teach you?

⌇ Recall at least one situation when you felt the tension of spending too lavishly on celebration, possibly at the cost of serving the needs of the poor and vulnerable?

Hospitality

All guests to the monastery should be welcomed as Christ, because He
will say, "I was a stranger, and you took me in."

Rule of Saint Benedict

A MEMORY COMES TO MIND from long ago—an experience of hospitality and welcoming I shall not forget.

In 1970, our family spent five months in Cuernavaca, Mexico, studying Spanish, and for the first four months of that stay we had pleasant accommodations. The *casa* we rented was one of three on a compound surrounded by a high wall with a lovely yard where our two toddlers could play safely with the six children of the caretakers. The oldest daughter, Tomasa, provided childcare for us, watching the children when we went off to study for the day, and the parents, Jose and Maria, conscientiously kept an eye on the property as well as the children. Their *casita* (little house) was the third one on the property, in no way comparable in size or comfort to the other two, one of which we occupied.

During these months we formed a warm friendship with this family, even as we struggled to communicate with our stilted and rudimentary command of the language at that time. We never met the wealthy family from Mexico City who owned the houses, but about ten days before Holy Week, we received a message from them. They informed us that their entire family planned to spend Holy Week at their country place in Cuernavaca, meaning the house we were renting, and would we vacate the premises, please.

This turn of events put is in a real bind. We intended to stay through the entire month to improve our Spanish just a bit more, but more seriously, it would be next to impossible for us to find another house to rent for such a short period, especially during Holy Week. We were upset about this situation and we found that Jose and Maria and their children were devastated that we were being treated this way. We talked about it and considered what we should do. We looked and they looked for an alternative, but neither of us found one.

Then one morning, the whole family appeared on our doorstep with broad smiles on their faces, announcing that they had a plan. We were anxious to hear what they had come up with.

"You can move into our small house for the week!" they said.

"No, No," we replied, "We couldn't possibly do that!"

"Oh, don't worry," they said. "We will fumigate it and even whitewash the walls!"

That was humbling. We didn't want to give them the impression that we were worried about the cleanliness of their house—for that wasn't the problem. But we had difficulty in communicating all this in Spanish.

"What would you do if we take over your house?" we asked.

Then they told us the happy solution that they had come up with.

"On the other side of the wall, there is an old shed," they said. "Years ago it was used for raising pigs, but now it's empty; so we can just move in there for the week, and you can have our house," they beamed.

That was the most hospitable offer we have ever received and one of the most delicate and difficult to turn down. It came from a poor family who wanted to give us their best, and it came from the heart.

I have wondered how hospitable we were in declining this incredible offer of hospitality. Perhaps we bungled it because we could not express our true feelings in Spanish at that time. It is interesting to remember that the rich drove us out, but the poor wanted to take action, hospitable action.

Reflection

The Benedictines have a simple and direct question ready for every sojourner and visitor who comes to the monastery. After assuring the visitor of a caring welcome in the peace of Christ, they ask, "Why have you come? What do you seek?" That is their greeting. In Viet Nam we used to walk around the village in the evenings exchanging greetings with our neighbors. In Vietnamese the polite greeting is expressed with the question, *Omg di dau?* Where are you going? In Spanish we say, *Como le va?* How goes it for you?

These are similar to the question Jesus asked two of his disciples one day. Jesus directed the question, "What are you looking for?" to the two disciples who were following him. Andrew said they were curious about where he was staying. Then Jesus said, "Come and see," and they stayed with him all that day. A good example of hospitality! The next day Jesus extended an invitation to them, saying, "Follow me."

It is always good to be welcomed. Being welcomed requires a generosity on the part of the welcomer. We must give of ourselves and take time to listen if we are to see Christ in the other.

Marjorie Thompson wrote about hospitality this way:

> Hospitality is essentially an expression of love. It is the act of sharing who we are as well as what we have. Thus, hospitality of the heart lies beneath every hospitable act. (*Soul Feast: an Invitation to the Christian Spiritual Life*, p. 122).

Meditation

Do not neglect to show hospitality to strangers, for by doing that some have entertained angels without knowing it.

Hebrews 13:2

☞ Recall a meaningful experience when you were graciously welcomed by others in a manner beyond your expectations. What made this experience so special?

☞ Think about your pattern of welcoming others. What do you take into account when making arrangements for those who visit you?

☞ Have you ever encountered Jesus in the form of a stranger? Describe this experience.

☞ What can you do to make sure your home, your church, and your workplace is welcoming and hospitable for others?

Mirth

*Mirth: A mood or temper characterized by joy and high spirits
and usually manifested in laughter and merrymaking.*

Ixil Triangle, Quiche Province, Guatemala, March 15, 2003

I have just spent a week in this paradise in the mountains of northern Guatemala.
This is the region where Agros International, with which I am now associated,
came to work with the *Ixil* (pronounced e-cheel) Indian people more than a
decade ago. It is called the *Ixil* triangle because three towns make up the points
of a triangle on the map where the heaviest concentration of the *Ixil* population
lives. The *Ixil* are one of the numerous ethnic groups who descended from the
Mayans of Central America and Southern Mexico. Their language is of Mayan
origin and is still maintained and spoken in all *Ixil* homes, though today the
men and children and some of the women also speak Spanish. Here the customs
and values arising out of their indigenous culture still provide guidance to daily
community life.

I feel privileged to be here to facilitate a training workshop with the *Ixil* leaders
and to hear their stories. Every one of them suffered through the period of
persecution, repression and violence in the 1980s. They refer to that as *la
violencia* (the time of violence). In the early '80s, the Guatemalan government,
under President Rios Mont, carried out scorched-earth warfare against whole
populations of indigenous peoples, especially in isolated areas like this, under the
false assumption that they were all subversives and guerillas. For almost 40 years
the government, controlled by the military, waged what amounted to class warfare
against their own people. The "enemy" was organized into several revolutionary
movements. It was a civil war in which tens of thousands of Indian people were

206

killed or forced to flee into the mountains or to southern Mexico as refugees.

This week all of the *Ixiles* in the workshop told stories of the massacres and attacks on their villages. The stories they told are familiar. I have visited many of these communities in the last several years and heard the accounts of these atrocities. The army swooped in, burning all the houses, killing the men and sometime women and children. Their livestock were taken and crops destroyed. Those who escaped fled into the forests and mountains and lived in fear for months or even years. During that long exile they suffered from intense hunger, disease and psychological trauma. Of course, some of the *Ixiles* did join the guerillas. They took up the armed struggle of defending themselves and their families. When the peace accords were signed in the 1990s, the people returned to their former homes but had little to return to. They had no houses, schools or tools, and often others had taken their land.

Their stories are peppered with the phrase *Gracias a Dios*, Thanks be to God (fill in the blank) "that we survived," "because we now live in peace," "that our families are safe," "for life," "for this help from Agros," etc. Even as they tell stories of their horrific past, they do so without bitterness. They have chosen not to live with hatred.

The mission of Agros is to help the *Ixil* rebuild their communities and lives. In many cases, Agros helps groups of families buy land to work and build completely new communities. It is amazing to be with these people and witness their devotion to God. They have an intense faith, testimony that suffering and hardship can build faith and a commitment to the way of peace. Their prayers are fervent. Most are Pentecostals, and their desire for a better future is unshakable, even as they continue for the present at a subsistence level of living.

They are also a people filled with joy and mirth. During the time of their forced exile they put their trust in God to deliver them from hatred and vengeance. They sang songs of praise and held their families and communities together. They found a way to laugh and sing even in the face of tragedy. Their exile is reminiscent to that of the Israelites:

> *By the rivers of Babylon—there we sat down and there we wept, when we remembered Zion. On the willows there we hung our harps. For there our*

captors asked us for songs, and our tormentors asked for mirth, saying, "Sing us one of the songs of Zion!" How could we sing the Lord's song in a foreign land? (Psalm 137:1–4).

The Ixil Triangle, Guatemala, Sept 22, 2005

I am back in the *Ixil* and sitting in a sparsely furnished little room in the town of Cotzal on the last evening of another workshop. I love being with these people—Guatemalans, Nicaraguans, Hondurans and Mexicans. Every night I retire to my room dead tired and happy. While I try to read before I fall asleep, I hear them in another room, talking and joking, but especially laughing and singing. Joy is a good word to describe this atmosphere, or maybe it is mirth. I feel delight in my heart to be with these down-to-earth Christians, eager to learn new skills and explore how to work with poor communities throughout Central America and Mexico. It is a privilege to be called on to lead training sessions with them. One of the things we learn is how to tell the stories and listen to each other.

Humor is always a good part of their stories. Some of the participants are leaders and promoters from villages; others are field workers and dedicated professionals. I am pleased that Agros has grown in maturity and capacity while at the same time maintaining a Christian mystique and identity. I am also thankful that the leadership has created a wide enough circle to include Evangelicals, Pentecostals, and Catholics. In the past I have seen too much of conflict and judgmental attitudes between these branches of the Church.

In the time we had together, we formed a deeply felt bond and love—sometimes we laughed so much our jaws tightened and bellies got sore. It was fun to be in a learning (and laughing) community like this. I think of one instance during the day that brings back a warm feeling.

We always try to be sure that everybody has understood what is being said, and we keep our language as straight forward and simple as possible. Some of the participants are barely literate, especially limited in Spanish comprehension; though that does not mean they are lacking in wisdom. And some of us are university-trained professionals, like agronomists and engineers.

During one session today Miguel got up his courage and said, *"No entiendo,"* (I don't understand). We immediately empathized and agreed, shaking our heads in affirmation. Of course! We should be more thoughtful. "But just ask Miguel," someone says. Not so easy for him to admit his lack of comprehension in a group of "*educados*" (educated people), when you are the least educated. Domingo got up and took the marker to record this finding on a flip chart. Domingo is very *educado*! He wrote out *Evitar Tecnocismos* (Avoid Technocisims). He had invented a new word—more jargon! We looked at each other for a few seconds and then burst out laughing. We have again caught ourselves being *demasiado educado—* (too educated!) Sometimes we just can't help ourselves.

As I look over the many pages of my journals and reflections on life and concerns on any given day, I am almost always serious, even sober, in my reflections about the spiritual life. In fact, as I look over the many books I have on my shelf concerning spirituality, prayer and the Christian life, I cannot point to any that deal in any significant way with humor, mirth and fun. But the word JOY appears many times in the Scriptures, and even this unfamiliar word, mirth, is occasionally found.

⟫◆⟪

I think back and try to remember the faces of my friends and colleagues in Central America, and I see them smiling and laughing. We talked and laughed a lot together. I am fluent in Spanish, and I have carried out meetings, discussions and workshops in Spanish for many years. But in a language that is not one's native tongue, it is difficult to understand the punch line of jokes. I have to admit that sometimes I would not get the joke. But laughter is so infectious that I would laugh out loud right along with the others, mostly because I enjoyed being caught up in the hilarity of the moment.

Now I vow to make a point to find something to laugh and smile about every day. Sometimes I even find myself chuckling in the middle of a prayer, and I think that's all right with God.

Reflection

In his book *A Hidden Wholeness*, Parker Palmer says that laughter can be as helpful as silence in bringing us closer to the sacred. He remembers a piece of wisdom that I also remember from a very early age, perhaps learned in the first grade—the admonition to laugh with people, not at them. Parker Palmer writes about the importance of this advice:

> That distinction came to mind when I learned that compassion literally means "feeling with" (p. 153).

> Compassionate laughter is the kind that emerges as we explore the shared human condition, where comedy is interwoven with tragedy. Laughing with each other is a form of compassion. . . . Silence and laughter may seem like strange bedfellows, but experience reveals that they are not. What, for example, do we call people who can spend hours together in silence without feeling awkward or tense and who can use humor to help each other through hard times? We call them, of course, good friends (p. 152).

Meditation

Blessed are you who are hungry now, for you will be filled.
Blessed are you who weep now, for you will laugh.

Luke 6:21

☞ What did you laugh about today? Did you laugh with someone else?

☞ Do you find Christians and the Church, in general, too serious? Or does humor attract you to congregate with other Christians?

☞ Think of examples you have seen of people suffering injustice or hardship. How did they use humor and laughter to help themselves get through difficulties?

☞ How have you used humor appropriately in situations of tension and even grief?

210

PART FIVE

Developing a Rule of Life

Many authors on subjects of spirituality and the spiritual life encourage us to live in the here-and-now. Each time I hear that phrase I remind myself of the wisdom of this principle, and with a pause and a deep breath, I consciously try to live in the moment. The truth is that we live between the past and the future. We build our lives on the legacy inherited from those who went before us, and we hope to leave something for those coming behind us. In reality we have no choice but to perpetually move into the future. As Thomas Carlyle said, "Go as far as you can see; when you get there you will be able to see farther."

To live fully in the present and maintain balance, we need both spontaneity and routine. We also need a certain amount of discipline. All the spiritual practices we have considered in previous chapters come together here as a framework for our ongoing spiritual lives, drawing on the past, living in the present and moving into the future. I refer to these as Cornerstones of Spirituality.

Legacy

*When you have eaten your fill and have built fine houses
and live in them, . . . and your silver and gold has multiplied
and all that you have is multiplied, then do not exalt yourself,
forgetting the Lord your God.*

Deuteronomy. 8:12–14

Tegucigalpa, Honduras, September 17, 1997

We are making the transition to live full-time back on our farm in Minnesota.
Judy is already there as I take off for Tegucigalpa from Little Rock, my second
trip to Honduras this year. She enjoys working outside, cleaning brush, the
accumulated branches and debris of the years. We are constantly dreaming and
planning for that place and our life on it. It has given us many good years and
pleasurable living already. We are happy to be "reclaiming" our place. It is part of
the legacy of my beloved parents and those before them.

My life is built on a legacy from the past. It was my parents and Aaker and Romo
grandparents who set me on my life path, and they in turn, from those who came
before them, all the way back to great-great grandparents Knut and Mari Aaker
who came to America in the 1840s. It was the land, the Church, the community
and the family, and even my cultural past from Norway and the settlement in
Minnesota that is the legacy and faith I inherited and which I feel obligated to
pass on to the next generation.

I read this quote somewhere: "I may not know who I am, but I know where I'm
from." I relate to that sentiment, though I think I have a strong sense both of who
I am and to whom I belong. What I keep struggling with is where I am going,
restless to do more, accomplish more, see and enjoy more of this world. Most of

214

my life I have been a misfit. I relish living and working in one place while at the same time thinking of other places I want to be and other things I dream of doing.

Mother Theresa died last week. Thank God for her good life, a life of dignity, love and humility; a witness to the world and to her Lord. She was one who certainly knew where she was meant to be. Her legacy will live on in the work of the Sisters of Charity, the order she established to minister to the poorest of the poor. Also this week, Princess Diana was killed in a car accident in Paris, and the whole world came to a standstill; practically a cult of deification formed as the masses mourned. What contrasting lives, but each in their own way left a mark and a legacy.

September 20, 1997

The Board of Directors of Heifer International is coming to Honduras to hold a meeting this week, the reason I have come. I was given responsibility for planning and facilitating this event and the related field trips. Several of my colleagues have arrived early, and we have a day before the board arrives. So we take advantage of this time to visit some old friends of Heifer who live in Honduras. We spent some time with two men who have long experience and have made an impact in the field of development. They happen to live in the same valley outside of Tegucigalpa.

Elias Sanchez has done much good with his life and has influenced many with his work in sustainable agriculture and community development. I recently read a book about his life and his vision of a sustainable farm. We visited his small model farm, and I was sorry to find that Elias is struggling with depression and looks like a worn-out and beaten man. Yet he showed some pride and satisfaction as he took us around to show us his place. His farm had recently taken a hit from heavy rains, and we could see the effects on the land and on Elias.

Talking quietly and recalling good memories of the past when he worked with Heifer, he gave thanks to God for the "little" he had accomplished. We listened and asked questions, trying to affirm him, but it is obvious that here is a man who is difficult to cheer up. I felt much empathy and compassion for Elias. Though not well known or recognized by the world, he is one who has been a good and faithful servant.

Next we visited Roland Bunch, well known in the world of development NGOs for his work in agriculture and for his book *Two Ears of Corn*. Roland has risen to the level of international expert in the development community and is in demand as a speaker at conferences and as a consultant in far flung places around the globe. In contrast to Elias, Roland was upbeat and talkative as he expounded on his work and theories of development. He did most of the talking, not pausing to inquire about us, as he had much to tell us, and of course, we were interested. I admit to some skepticism of experts whose experience attracts so much attention. I recognize that such people have much to offer, and I cannot deny that Roland will leave a good legacy, and his impact is likely to continue into the future.

In 1 Corinthians 3, Paul writes about building our lives on a foundation that will stand the test of fire. I hope that the Board of Directors gathered here chooses wisely as they build on the wisdom of the past and make decisions for the future. The founders of Heifer Project International left a legacy that they could not have imagined, a program that benefited millions and has continued to pass on the gift of hope and life for over 50 years.

Siguatepeque, Honduras, *June 23, 2003*

I am at the home of my good friends, Norma and Enrique Martinez. Norma and I work together in Agros International and Enrique is the Director of the Evangelical Hospital in this town. Norma and I will be co-leading an orientation seminar for the new staff of Agros from around Central America. Norma and I complement each other and work well together. If I have had any success in all my years of work in Latin America, one of the secrets is this—always team up with a Latin American colleague, in this case Norma, as a co-trainer.

As I traveled here yesterday, I wondered why I am still doing this, traveling, working, being absent from Judy and the farm. This is a good time of the year to be at home on the farm. I would rather be there. But today some excitement started to grow within me as I re-engaged with Agros again in Central America. My motivation returned and melancholy faded.

216

Honduras, June 25, 2003

As a part of the training of new staff, we made a visit to a rural community called Germanias II. This was a good place to see the reality of why we are doing what we are doing, another encounter with poverty. Most of the women and some of the men are illiterate, and many work in nearby coffee farms for $2.50 a day, live on corn and beans, have no animals, little land to cultivate, and of what little they grow there is no excess to sell. All the families have from three to five children, and with no money, they have little prospect of sending their children to education beyond the first grades in the local elementary school. They will have no material legacy to leave their children. They hope their love and sacrifice is sufficient and that their children will be better off than they are.

How do I feel and react to this condition of poverty and underdevelopment after having worked in programs to end hunger and alleviate poverty for over 35 years? To be honest, at times I am tired, and a feeling of hopelessness invades my spirit. On the one hand despair but on the other hand a feeling of hope and encouragement. Why? I see this new generation of motivated people, young idealistic Central Americans, replacing us of the older generation, and I want to give my best to transmit something of my experience and learning to them.

San Pedro Sula, Honduras, June 27, 2003

The workshop is finished, and the Guatemalans and Nicaraguans have departed for their respective homes. The most important things we try to transmit to these recently hired staff are the values that underpin our work with the communities: participation, respect and accountability, amongst others. Values and "people skills" are at the core of what we do in community development. In a three-day workshop, we can detect which of these young people have the capacity and/or natural ability to facilitate with, rather than do for, the communities. It went well, and I am confident they will do well, though there are, as always, doubts about whether one or two of the participants really understood the essence of our key message.

I am staying at the Bolivar Hotel, which was my home away from home almost 30 years ago when I was working in the humanitarian emergency created by

Hurricane Fifi in 1974. I reminisce. We were living in Nicaragua, supported by Lutheran World Relief and representing Church World Service in the disaster response. I was 34 years old and had gone to Nicaragua in early 1973 after the Christmas Eve earthquake of 1972—sent there to work with the churches of Nicaragua to set up an effective emergency response, which became, within a few years, a long-term development program all over the country.

In 1974 I came here many times to coordinate the response of U.S. churches and to establish an organization of Honduran churches. Thirty-four years old seems very young to me now, but Judy and I had already spent two years in Vietnam, three in Peru and two in Nicaragua involved in disasters and community development, so we had a bit of experience. I must have had more energy in those days and perhaps a bit of naïve optimism. To be frank and objectively realistic, I am sure I would not assume such overwhelming challenges again these days.

This hotel is exactly the same as I remember it, rather dingy and damp. They have not done a thing to renovate or improve it. I might be sitting in the same chair I sat in 28 years ago. Names and faces come back to me—Gus from the United Church of Christ; Oscar, a local businessman; Neomi, a dynamic woman leader from the Reformed Church; Ovideo, a Mennonite; and Tim and Gloria, all still good friends after all these years. Back home, I have many slides in a box that document the hurricane's destruction and the reconstruction efforts we worked on. I need to look for them sometime.

Life has passed by quickly. I now find myself back here but in a completely different context with a completely different job, pleased to be working with motivated young people. We keep at it, trying to train, orient and transmit to them some of what we have learned, a part of the legacy of my generation to the next.

Reflection

Do you wonder about doing the will of God in your life and leaving a legacy? Jesus gave us a way to test this when he said, *Anyone who resolves to do the will of God will know whether the teaching is from God or whether I am speaking on my own.* (John 7:17) Even if I am resolved to do the will of God, it is not always clear or easy to discern that will. I may be striving after my own glory. These are good questions to ponder: As we grow older and gain some degree of experience and reputation, how do we best share real wisdom and do it with dignity and humility?

Meditation

The boundary lines have fallen for me in pleasant places;
I have a goodly heritage. . . . You show me the path of life.
In your presence there is fullness of joy; in your right hand
are pleasures forevermore.

Psalm 16:6, 11

☞ At whatever point you may be in your life's work, think back on your ministry and service in the world. What words would you use to describe how you feel about your life's work so far?

☞ Our lives are never lived in a vacuum; we are part of history. Given your unique history, focus on what legacies were foundational for your life?

☞ When all is said and done, what do you want your legacy to be? What have been your deepest joys? Your greatest concerns?

Vision

Where there is no prophecy, the people cast off restraint.
Proverbs 29:18

For many years I worked with organizations in a rather exciting process of defining values and vision. Sometimes the people I worked with would forget what their agreed upon core values and visions were. I was always curious about that. When I asked them to name their vision and values a few months after our workshop, they would give a blank stare, as if I was asking them to describe their sex life. I would stress to them the importance of remembering their vision and values, not just writing them into a planning document. The challenge is how to express these values and live out our vision in daily life and work. The New Jerusalem Bible translates the above verse as *Where there is no vision the people get out of hand.* We were aiming at keeping on track—and not getting out of hand!

Having a vision and being able to articulate it pulls us forward, motivates us and gives us inspiration for the future. Look at what it meant for the civil rights movement in the United States to have heard the speech by Dr. Martin Luther King, Jr. entitled "I Have a Dream!" That may be the only line of the speech we can repeat from memory, but it lives on in the memory of millions.

As I look back at my own vision, I see that the first pages of my journal from 1997 are filled with notes about dreams for our farm and the life we would live there.

At home on the farm, *January, 1997*

Usually I make resolutions for the New Year, writing specific goals for the upcoming year. Next January I will look back to see what I wrote and what I did or did not achieve. Even though I may not refer to this list throughout the year, this practice does commit a few ideas to the conscious and unconscious memory bank.

I have a desire to start anew, to strip away the old self and live on the land as those who lived here before me, to get back to my roots. My plans are to plant many trees and a garden, put up fences for animals we will raise on our farm, build a small cabin that can be my hermitage, sow my fields with grass where the livestock will graze and build a small barn. Judy and I have talked a lot about our hopes for our farm, and in thinking about a vision statement I penned this phrase: "To live in harmony with the Spirit of God in this place, and with the natural world, neighbors and each other."

Jesus said, *The Kingdom of God is like treasure hidden in a field, which someone found and hid; then in his joy he goes and sells all he has and buys that field* (Matthew 13:44). I think the point here is the joy of discovering the most important life treasures.

February, 1997

I am at the Heifer International ranch in Arkansas to run a workshop on sustainable agriculture for farmers, field staff and extension agents from all over the South. This is a diverse group of women, and men, including many black farmers, plus the young and idealistic staff. As I ended the first day in this normally quiet place, many sounds and impressions echoed in my mind: laughter, plenty of discussion and good-natured banter. And from my room in the lodge I hear the African Americans from Louisiana talking to each other late into the night.

We have been working on values and vision in our Heifer program model as we strive to help farmers and communities plan for the future. I posed the question, "What kind of a life do you want to live on your farm, in your family, and in your community or organization? What is most important in life to you?"

One of the speakers today was Joel Salitan, well-known in the sustainable farming community. He talked with evangelistic fervor about his family and the quality of life they strive for on their farm in Virginia. Their goal is to have "an emotionally satisfying and economically fruitful life that enhances the environment and shares with the world." His vision is big and boundless. He looks forward 20–30 years to the next generation. And he can name his vision and talk about how it looks now and how it will look in the future because he and his family are already on the way, and they are in the process of being molded and formed toward that future he envisions for their farm.

Rosa, one of the Muslim women in our group, talked about the intentional community in Alabama of which she is a part. She said this about the vision for their community, which they call New Medina, "It is to be a place where God is pleased to abide." What a nicely phrased goal and vision . . . one which any Christian or Muslim could easily embrace. In the midst of my seemingly endless pondering about what might be a good vision for our own farm, I put this one into the mix, "To create a place where God is pleased to abide."

When I look back at the dreams that Judy and talked about in 1997, I realize that these ideals were a mixture of fantasy and hopes along with other realistic and attainable goals.

Is it disappointing to look back on life and see that some of our dreams remain unfulfilled? Do unaccomplished goals mean failure? Maybe, but I don't really think so. It might also be cause for dissatisfaction when we realize that we fall short of the ideals of Christian living. But again we can be relieved of that burden. St. Paul wrote about the behaviors and attributes of the Christian life in the third chapter of Colossians:

> *Clothe yourselves in compassion, kindness, meekness and patience . . . forgive each other. Above all clothe yourselves with love, which binds everything together in perfect harmony* (Colossians 3:12, 15).

In this passage we see that clothing ourselves in love (choosing this garment) means that God's purpose is revealed in us—success, failure and legacy become less important.

222

Reflection

The future is not totally predictable, and our vision may propel us into an uncertain future. In his book about Henri Nouwen, Will Hernandez wrote about Nouwen's continuous search throughout his life, "Constantly in life we get pulled in either one of two directions: are we to stay put here where we are or to launch out on an uncharted territory" (*A Spirituality of Imperfection*, p. 105).

Our values come from several sources. Some we inherit from the culture into which we are born, from parents, teachers, and our church, or from other inspiring figures. Others are discovered along the way and become our own as we mature and find our path in life. Our culture can also instill "anti-values," such as self-indulgence, materialism and egotism.

Keeping mindful of God and the Scriptures, we are reminded of spiritual values— the fruits of the Spirit—by which to live. We are also warned of those things that draw us away from God, the spiritual life and the discovery of our true selves.

Meditation

In the last days it will be, God declares, that I will pour out my spirit on all flesh, and your sons and your daughters will prophesy, and your young men will see visions, and your old men shall dream dreams.

Acts 2:17

☞ What core values guide you in your life and work?

☞ Can you articulate the vision of the organization or group with which you work? What values are foundational to the program and mission of your organization?

☞ If possible, discuss the topic of values and vision with members of your church or the organization with which you work. Are you on the same wave length regarding a common vision?

Cornerstones of Spirituality

A rule of life . . . fosters gifts of the Spirit in personal life and human community, helping to form us into the persons God intends us to be.

Marjorie Thompson

THE FOUNDERS OF ORDERS AND MONASTERIES, such as Saint Benedict, wrote a "rule of life" for those who joined the community. This Rule describes attitudes and specific practices that guide monks in their common life. These directives are still followed in Benedictine monasteries today. Outside of the cloistered life, many priests, nuns and pastors follow the readings and prayers in a Daily Office or Prayer Book throughout the liturgical year and set aside time for personal retreats and spiritual direction. These disciplines are not limited to the clergy or those living in cloistered communities, of course, and I know a few lay people who are disciplined enough to spend an hour or more a day in prayer and meditation.

Perhaps you feel drawn to a spirituality of service and are interested in developing a rule of life for yourself. If you are involved in outreach and social action, your days are already filled with much activity. When the desire or inclination to deepen your spiritual life is incorporated into this activism, it is obvious that you may practice your spirituality on the run. Or, if you are like me, you give attention to spiritual practices when you have time. This often means putting it on hold or at a lower priority than you would like. Spiritual practices like worship, contemplative silence and daily prayer may seem desirable but elusive, to be put off until later when you have some *extra* time or energy.

The most common excuse for not making a commitment to daily spiritual practice is "I don't have enough time." However, it is unlikely that we will deepen our relationship with God in a casual or haphazard manner. Everyone has the same amount of time every day—1,440 minutes.

If you feel the desire to establish a better balance and focus in life, the following is offered as a process for analysis, discernment and possibly as a way to help you develop your own rule of life.

One approach with which I have much familiarity is the concept of cornerstones—a mixture of values, principles and practices that are found to be building blocks of a successful project, program or organization. This approach can be applied to family, community or individual life, as well, and I believe it is also relevant to the spiritual life. Some of the organizations I worked with defined these essential components as a kind of checklist to keep in mind when planning, managing and evaluating a project or the functioning of an organization. It is a way to live out our values and actually do what we say we believe. In other words, it is a way to live an integrated life.

One caveat about cornerstones: though we may define these practices, values and principles as important for an effective and successful project or spiritual life, we must accept as a given that all cornerstones are not equal, or at least they are not all equally possible to implement.

It may be useful for you to develop a list of spiritual cornerstones to keep yourself balanced and on track in order to live out your spirituality. Your cornerstones could be thought of as your rule of life. Obviously, every person has to develop a list that is uniquely their own. It is sometimes instructional and inspirational to read the list of a giant of faith and action, like St. Benedict or Mother Theresa, but I must pray as I can and not as I can't. The point for me is that I need a standard to live up to. Living a life dedicated to serve those who are in need and vulnerable demands focus and discipline.

Here is a list of some possible cornerstones for a spiritual life: (these are mine and listed as examples).

Prayer—A time of quiet in the early morning to stretch and pray while the mind is not cluttered. This is a time for the body to wake up, for the lungs to expand through deep breathing and for the heart to be receptive to the Spirit. Sometimes I extend this to include time for silence or journaling. This practice can be done in the quietness of your home, but it could also be carried out while on an early morning walk or bike ride. For me this takes about twenty minutes.

Consider this: Where, how and when can you find time for prayer and quietness? Do you or can you set aside intentional time and space for prayer and quiet? When is the best time of the day for you? An excellent resource for the practice mentioned above is the book by Murray D. Finck, *Stretch and Pray: A Daily Discipline for Physical and Spiritual Wellness,* listed in the bibliography.

Meditation on the Word—Every morning after breakfast, Judy and I read a portion of Scripture and reflect on the text. We use a devotional resource with texts from the Common Lectionary that leads to short prayers of intercession for needs that are suggested or others that come to mind. Dietrich Bonhoeffer wrote: "It is not necessary that we should get through an entire passage in one meditation. Often we stop with one sentence or even one word. It is not necessary for us to express our thoughts and prayers in words. Un-phrased thought and prayer which issues only from our hearing may often be more beneficial" (*Life Together*, p. 73). Often these words stay with us the whole day long.

Consider this: If you don't now read Scripture regularly, what about starting by reading just one or two verses each day? "Chewing" on The Word in small bites can be edifying. The ancient method of lectio divina, described in the book by Thelma Hall listed in the bibliography, is an excellent resource on this subject. Daily devotional resources are available from most church denominations.

Worship—I need to be regularly connected to the community—the Body of Christ—through the liturgy and Eucharist. I believe it is difficult to be a private Christian. We need the Word and Sacrament and fellowship. Participation in the Church, with all its blemishes, both supports and challenges me; it keeps me accountable to and supportive of both a particular congregation and the Church around the world.

Consider this: Examine your commitment to regular worship. If you currently do not desire to participate in worship with others, what are your reasons? Do you go to church to get something out of the service, or are you there to praise and worship God and be fed by word and sacrament in preparation for going out into the world to serve? You may wish to refer to the chapter in this book on worship and use the questions for deeper reflection. If you have dropped out of corporate worship, talk about your feelings and reasons with a pastor or a friend who does participate in a congregation.

Seeking Justice and Peace—Although current events are often overwhelming and frustrating, we try to keep up, especially with issues that affect people who are hungry, those who live in poverty and our deteriorating environment. The challenge is to turn our concerns into action. For hunger policy issues, Judy and I support Bread for the World financially and by writing letters to our representatives and senators. We also support several other advocacy groups. There are many good causes, but homework and checking the track record and stewardship of each is important. One place to start is to visit www.guidestar.org.

Consider this: While the issues and needs are many, have you prioritized what is most important to you and focused your attention on these issues? Think of specific ways to turn your concerns into action. It is better to join with other like-minded and motivated people and work together lest you become frustrated and pessimistic about the possibility that you can make a difference in the face of such great needs and disparities. This prioritization and intentionality will help you feel less guilty about saying no to many other excellent organizations.

Service—Even though I am retired and no longer work full time in a service organization, I can still find places to be of service. Locally, I can serve as a volunteer in the church and community, such as a community garden, a community foundation and a social ministry of the church. There are many excellent international and local organizations for poverty alleviation and long-term community development. Because of prior experience, Judy and I have confidence in and support several humanitarian and service programs financially.

Consider this: If you are discerning a career choice or a change of direction, investigate and read about projects or organizations to which you are attracted. What are some opportunities for service close to home right now? What are your gifts? Talk to people who are or have worked in the field of service in which you are interested. This is certainly where the principle "watch for the will of God" comes into play. Be open to the possibility of being the right person at the right time and in the right place. It just might happen. Pray for discernment of God's will for your life.

Contemplation and Silence—There can be ample opportunities throughout every day to reflect on experience in the light of faith and to take some time for silence. These moments might include the spontaneous flaring up of praise for creation while on a walk; gratitude for health and family; contemplative time in a peaceful and silent setting; and prayers for others in need as they come into your consciousness at unexpected moments. Contemplative (silent) prayer with a group can also be consoling.

Consider this: If your life is full of demands and interruptions, what can you do to structure time for silence and contemplation? Instead of turning on the television or computer for outside stimulus, try solitude and mindfulness of the Divine presence during your daily activities. Look again at the chapters on silence and contemplation in this book and the books listed in the bibliography. Browse through books on contemplation and meditation in a bookstore and read one that attracts your attention. However, it is important that you start practicing silence in an intentional way. Just reading about it is not sufficient.

Sharing and Caring—This cornerstone prompts us to be mindful of the needs of those around me, ordinary courtesy, listening carefully in daily conversations and small acts of kindness. I am challenged in daily life to accept people who are different from me in values, traditions, appearance and beliefs. I need to be watchful for the onset of a judgmental attitude.

Consider this: Who are those in your daily life you can and should care for? Where are you most challenged to stretch in your caring and sharing for others? Be mindful of the needs of others and aware of attitudes that keep you from loving others as fully as you would like. Practice mindfulness.

Spiritual Direction—For periods of time I have had a spiritual director for individual sessions once a month as well as participating in group spiritual direction. Spiritual direction is sometimes difficult to arrange, depending on where one lives.

Consider this: Who gives you support and feedback about your spiritual life? Do you have or would you like to find a spiritual director or soul friend to talk with on a regular basis? Try to find a support group or prayer group with whom you can share your concerns and blessings. Talk to a trusted person, perhaps a pastor or lay leader, about this desire. Find out if there are trained spiritual directors in your area. Several resources are included in the Bibliography to explain spiritual direction and its benefits. Find more information at spiritual directors international.org.

I don't do all of the above spiritual cornerstones well every day, though there are some days when the Spirit gives much consolation and fulfillment. Those who are close to me in my daily life can attest to the reality of my failure to fully achieve these ideals on any given day.

As I have tried to point out, self-awareness is a first step, for the spiritual life is intricately fused with the everyday and ordinary stuff of our lives. Henri Nouwen reminds us that our busy lives make it hard for us to free up time and space for God. I have noticed this in myself as well as in the lives of others who pursue a call to service.

Certainly it is essential to have a balance of activities for mind, body and spirit. There is a time for introspection and a time for action; a time for private prayer and a time for common prayer; a time to do and a time to be.

Reflection

Douglas V. Steere says there are some plain rules of spiritual hygiene concerning prayer. He writes:

> The first of these rules is that, in order to pray, you have to stop being too elsewhere and be there.

> You have to care enough so that you will collect yourself, move back into your own soul from the distant suburbs where much of life tends to be spent, and honestly be there (*Dimensions of Prayer*, p. 13).

What does being there mean for you? Where has your journey taken you? That is a question I have explored in this book and one that can only be answered by each individual on his or her own journey. May God go with you on your way!

Meditation

So then you are no longer strangers and aliens,
but you are citizens with the saints and also members
of the household of God, built upon the foundation
of the apostles and prophets, with Christ Jesus himself
as the cornerstone.

Ephesians 2:19

☞ Take some time now to reflect on the above list of eight Spiritual Cornerstones and then write your own list. Include those practices and attitudes that you now hold to, as well as some new ones you think you might want to follow more seriously in your life someday soon.

☞ If you wrote your own definition of spirituality before you began reading this book, take a look at that now. Having read and considered the ideas in this book, what of your original definition would you keep and what would you change?

☞ Finally, in what ways do you feel God's Spirit is prompting you to stretch and grow in your own journey?

Closing Challenge:
and "What About You?"

Years ago when I was a student at Luther College, we were required to attend daily chapel. That meant I listened to about 500 chapel talks during those years. I don't remember any specific details of those meditations, but I do recall the deep commitment to faithfulness and the passion for service expressed by those many pastors and teachers who shared their wisdom and their life stories with us students. Memories of encounters with those and other caring and questioning mentors along the way continue to influence me to this day as I live out my life of faith and service.

At the conclusion of each of his talks, Pastor Gordon Selbo always finished with this question: "And what about you?" He wanted to bring the message and the Scripture text right back to us and challenge us to ponder its meaning for our lives.

You may have come to this last page of the book having nibbled and snacked on just a few of my stories and reflections, or you may have partaken in the full course and read it all. Either way, I hope you have been impacted by the people to whom you have been introduced, and that the stories and reflections I have shared in these pages have drawn a picture of what it has meant for me to walk with the poor in spirit and in service.

However, let's be clear, your hearing my journey is not the most critical issue. The important question is, "What about you?" In what ways are you answering for yourself the questions at the end of each chapter? How have you worked out your own answers to the questions about life's meaning, purpose and calling? In what ways do you continue to ask and answer, to discern and respond, as you craft your own understanding of how you are called to the dual challenges of spirituality and service—as you live out your life?

Blessings on your journey.

Glossary of Organizations

Agros International (AI) www.agros.org: Based in Seattle, Washington, Agros International is committed to breaking the cycle of poverty for rural families in Central America and Mexico by enabling landless communities to achieve land ownership and economic stability. For about eight years (2000–2008) after my retirement, I worked part-time for Agros as a trainer and advisor for Central American staff.

Bread for the World (BFW) www.bread.org: "Bread" is a collective Christian voice urging our nation's decision-makers to end hunger at home and abroad. Bread for the World members send personal letters and emails, and they meet with members of Congress to urge support for just policies and programs that benefit the poor and hungry at home and abroad. My wife, Judy, and I have been Bread members for over 30 years.

Church World Service (CWS) www.churchworldservice.org: CWS, founded in 1946, is a cooperative ministry of 35 Christian denominations and communions in the United States, providing sustainable self-help, development, disaster relief and refugee assistance. While not employed by CWS, we worked in close collaboration with CWS in Vietnam, Peru and Central America.

The Evangelical Church in America (ELCA) www.elca.org: The ELCA was formed in 1988 from three separate and well-established North American church bodies, one of which was the Lutheran Church in America (LCA). Judy and I served as missionaries with the LCA in Peru for three years between 1969 and 1972. We are members of a congregation of the ELCA.

Heifer International (HI) www.heifer.org: Heifer, founded in 1944, is a nonprofit charitable organization rooted in the Quaker/Brethren tradition. Now based in Little Rock, Arkansas, HI is dedicated to relieving global hunger and poverty. It provides gifts of livestock and plants, as well as education in sustainable agriculture, to financially-disadvantaged families around the world. I worked for Heifer for over 16 years, primarily as Program Director for Latin America and the Caribbean in the 1980s and as Director of Training in the 1990s. HI was formerly called Heifer Project International (HPI).

Lutheran World Relief (LWR) www.lwr.org: LWR, headquartered in Baltimore, Maryland, is the relief and development agency of Lutherans in the United States. LWR is sponsored and supported by the Evangelical Lutheran Church in America and the Lutheran Church-Missouri Synod. LWR's mission statement reads: "Affirming God's love for all people, we work with Lutherans and other partners around the world to end poverty, injustice and human suffering." Judy and I worked for over twelve years for LWR, in Vietnam (1966–68), in Central American (1973–78) and in the Andean Region of South America (1988–91). I also represented LWR part-time on a traveling basis in Central America between 1979 and 1987.

Mennonite Central Committee (MCC), www.mcc.org: Founded in 1920, MCC is a relief, service, and peace agency representing 15 Mennonite, Brethren in Christ and Amish bodies in North America. We worked closely with MCC volunteers and programs in Vietnam and Central America.

Bibliography

Arnold, Eberhard. *When the Time Was Fulfilled*, reprinted in *Watch for the Light: Readings for Advent and Christmas*, Farmington, PA: Plough Publishing House, 2001. Used by permission.

Borg, Marcus. *Meeting Jesus Again for the First Time*, San Francisco: Harper, 1994. Used by permission.

Bonhoeffer, Dietrich. *Life Together,* London: SCM Press, LTD, 1954. Used by permission.

Britts, Phillip. "Yielding to God," an unpublished address given in 1949, reprinted in *Watch for the Light: Readings for Advent and Christmas*, Farmington, PA: Plough Publishing House, 2001. Used by permission.

Dear, John. *Living Peace: A Spirituality of Contemplation and Action*, New York: Image Books/Doubleday, 2001.

Edwards, Tilden. *Spiritual Director, Spiritual Companion: Guide to Tending the Soul*, New York: Paulist Press, 2001. Used by permission.

Goodall, Jane. *Reason for Hope: A Spiritual Journey*, New York: Warner Books, 1999.

Hanson, Bradley C. *A Graceful Life: Lutheran Spirituality for Today*, Minneapolis, Augsburg Fortress, 2000. Used with permission.

Hernandez, Wil. *Henri Nouwen: A Spirituality of Imperfection*, Copyright © 2006 by The Leadership Institute, Paulist Press, Inc.: New York/Mahwah, N.J. Used with permission of Paulist Press. www.paulistpress.com

_____. *Henri Nouwen and Soul Care: A Ministry of Integration*. Copyright © 2008 by The Leadership Institute. Paulist Press, Inc.: New York/Mahwah, N.J. Used with permission of Paulist Press. www.paulistpress.com

Huggett, Joyce. *Learning the Language of Prayer*, New York: Crossroad, 1997.

Kelly, Thomas R. *A Testament of Devotion*, San Francisco: Harper & Brothers, 1941. Used by permission.

Kidd, Sue Monk. *When the Heart Waits*, San Francisco: Harper, 1992. Used by permission.

May, Gerald G. *The Dark Night of the Soul: A Psychiatrist Explores the Connection Between Darkness and Spiritual Growth*, San Francisco: Harper, 2004. Used by permission.

Nouwen, Henri J. *Gracias! A Latin American Journal*, San Francisco: Harper & Row, 1983. Used by permission

_____. *The Genesee Dairy: Report from a Trappist Monastery*, New York: Image Books, 1989.

_____. *The Return of the Prodigal Son: A Story of Homecoming*, New York: Image Books, 1994.

_____, Donald P McNeill, and Douglas A Morrison, *Compassion: Reflections on the Christian Life*, New York: Doubleday, 1982. Used by permission of Doubleday, a division of Random House, Inc.

_____. *Making All Things News*, San Francisco: Harper, San Francisco, 1981. Used by permission.

Palmer, Parker J. *A Hidden Wholeness: The Journey Toward an Undivided Life*, San Francisco: Jossey-Bass, 2004. This material (quote) is reproduced with permission of John Wiley & Sons, Inc.

_____. *Let Your Life Speak: Listening for the Voice of Vocation*, San Francisco: Jossey-Bass, Publishers, 2000. Quoted material is reproduced with permission of John Wiley & Sons, Inc.

Reeves, Nancy. *I'd Say Yes, God, If I Knew What You Wanted*. Copyright © 2001 Nancy Reeves, Northstone Publishing, an imprint of Wood Lake Publishing Inc., Kelowna, BC, Canada. Used by permission.

Schmidt, Joseph F. *Praying Our Experiences*, Winona, MN: Saint Mary's Press, 1980. *Quotes are from Praying Our Experiences* by Joseph Schmidt, FSC, copyright © 2008, The Word Among Us Press, Frederick, Maryland, www.wau. org. Used with permission.

Steere, Douglas V. *Dimensions of Prayer*, Nashville: Upper Room, revised edition, 1997. Used with permission.

Sztehlo, Gabor. *In the Hands of God*, Budapest: Published by the Gabor Sztehlo Foundation for the help of Children and Adolescents, 1994. Used with permission.

Thompson, Marjorie J. *Soul Feast: An Invitation to the Christian Spiritual Life*, Louisville: Westminster John Knox Press, 1995. Quotes are from *Soul Feast: An Invitation to the Christian Spiritual Life.* © 1995 Marjorie J. Thompson. Used by permission of Westminster John Knox Press.

Vennard, Jane E. *A Praying Congregation*, Herndon, VA: The Alban Institute, 2005. Used with permission.

Other Resources on Prayer and Spirituality

Barry, William A. SJ. *Discernment in Prayer: Paying Attention to God*, Notre Dame, Indiana: Ave Maria Press, 1990.

Dougherty, Rose Mary SSND. *Group Spiritual Direction: Community for Discernment*, New York: Paulist Press, 1995.

Edwards, Tilden. *Spiritual Friend: Reclaiming the Gift of Spiritual Direction.* New York: Paulist Press, 1980.

Finck, Murray D. *Stretch and Pray: A Daily Discipline for Physical and Spiritual Wellness*, Minneapolis: Augsburg Books, 2005.

Hall, Thelma. *Too Deep for Words: Rediscovering Lectio Divina*, New York: Paulist Press, 1988.

Main, John. *Moment of Christ: The Path of Meditation*, New York: Continuum, 1999.

Meninger, William A. *The Loving Search for God: Contemplative Prayer and the Cloud of Unknowing*, New York: Continuum Publishing, 1995.

Merton, Thomas. *Spiritual Direction and Meditation*, Collegeville, Minnesota: The Liturgical Press, 1960.

Morris, Danny E, and Charles Olsen. *Discerning God's Will Together: A Spiritual Practice for the Church*, Bethesda: Alban Publications, 1997.

Nouwen, Henri. *The Way of the Heart*, New York: Harper Collins, 1991.

Nouwen, Henri, Michael Christensen, and Rebecca J Laird. *Spiritual Direction: Wisdom for the Long Walk of Faith*, San Francisco: Harpers, 2006.

Pennington, M. Basil. *Lectio Divina: Renewing the Ancient Practice of Praying the Scriptures*, New York: The Crossroads Publishing Company, 1998.

Wicks, Robert J. *Everyday Simplicity: A Practical Guide to Spiritual Growth*, Notre Dame, Indiana: Sorin Books, 2000.

Wicks, Robert J. *Snow Falling on Snow*, New York: Paulist Press, 2010.

Appreciation

Thanks to Judy, my wife, and our children, Bret, Lani and Daniel for their love and acceptance. Thanks to Janis Hansen, Val Neeley, Al Heggen, Donald Tubesing, Doug Smith and Florence Ore for reading the manuscript and for valuable feedback and encouragement. Also, a word of appreciation is due to Anna Bedford for her excellent editing and insightful suggestions. To one of my heroes in the world of advocacy on behalf of the hungry and poor, thanks to Art Simon for his words.

My appreciation also goes to many friends, colleagues, mentors and spiritual companions with whom I worked and learned in myriad situations through the years. They came from various countries, faith traditions and vocations: Bob Busch, Peter Lindberg, Gustavo Parajon, Gordon Hatcher, Susan Stewart, Darrell Huddelston, Jim De Vries, Pedro Velez, Gregory Rake, Eduardo Sotomayor, Marlyn Sundheim, Dwight Schwartzendruber and Jennifer Shumaker are several of the friends and colleagues with whom I worked for long periods of time during some of the most challenging periods of my career in international service.

Finally, I owe an immense debt of appreciation to hundreds of community leaders and colleagues from partner organizations. Also, to small-scale farmers and people living in poverty in rural and urban settings: women and men, youth and children, whom I had the privilege of knowing in more than forty countries to which my journey of service took me during the course of four decades.

As I was finishing the manuscript of this book, I met Don Tubesing through a mutual friend—certainly a serendipitous encounter. For some time, Don had been thinking about and discerning the possibility of re-entering the publishing business and had arrived at the idea of launching a series of books entitled *Wisdom from the Elders: Giving Voice to the Deepest Insights of Our Most Experienced Citizens*. After reading the manuscript, he proposed that Pfeifer-Hamilton publish my book as the initial title in this series. Thanks Don and thanks be to God for answer to prayer.